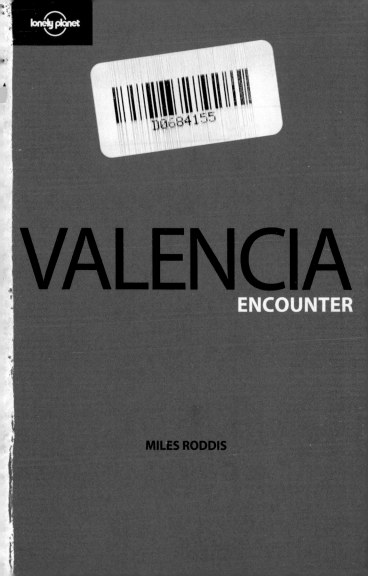

lonely planet

D0684155

VALENCIA
ENCOUNTER

MILES RODDIS

Valencia Encounter

Published by Lonely Planet Publications Pty Ltd
ABN 36 005 607 983

Australia	Locked Bag 1, Footscray,
(Head Office)	Vic 3011
	☎ 03 8379 8000 fax 03 8379 8111
	talk2us@lonelyplanet.com.au
USA	150 Linden St, Oakland, CA 94607
	☎ 510 250 6400
	toll free 800 275 8555
	fax 510 893 8572
	info@lonelyplanet.com
UK	2nd fl, 186 City Rd
	London EC1V 2NT
	☎ 020 7106 2100 fax 020 7106 2101
	go@lonelyplanet.co.uk

This title was commissioned in Lonely Planet's London
office and produced by: **Commissioning Editors** Korina
Miller, Lucy Monie **Coordinating Editors** Charlotte
Harrison, Alison Ridgway **Coordinating Cartographer**
Jacqueline Nguyen **Layout Designer** Carlos Solarte
Assisting Cartographers Fatima Basic, Xavier Di Toro,
Joanne Luke **Managing Editor** Sasha Baskett **Senior Edi-
tor** Katie Lynch **Managing Cartographer** David Connolly
Managing Layout Designer Laura Jane **Cover** Image
Research provided by lonelyplanetimages.com **Project
Manager** Chris Girdler **Thanks to** Mark Griffiths, Aomi
Hongo, Rachel Imeson, Indra Kilfoyle, Herman So, Lyahna
Spencer, Clifton Wilkinson

ISBN 978 1 74104 813 1

Printed through Colorcraft Ltd, Hong Kong.
Printed in China.

Acknowledgment Valencia Metro Map © 2009.

HOW TO USE THIS BOOK
Colour-Coding & Maps

Colour-coding is used for symbols on maps and in
the text that they relate to (eg all eating venues on
the maps and in the text are given a green knife and
fork symbol). Each neighbourhood also gets its own
colour, and this is used down the edge of the page
and throughout that neighbourhood section.

Shaded yellow areas on the maps denote areas
of interest – for their historical significance, their
attractive architecture or their great bars and restaurants. We encourage you to head to these areas
and just start exploring!

Prices

Multiple prices listed with reviews (eg €10/5 or
€10/5/20) indicate adult/child, adult/concession
or adult/child/family.

Send us your feedback We love to hear from
readers – your comments help make our books better. We read every word you send us, and we always
guarantee that your feedback goes straight to the
appropriate authors. The most useful submissions are
rewarded with a free book. To send us your updates
and find out about Lonely Planet events, newsletters
and travel news visit our award-winning website:
lonelyplanet.com/contact.

Note: We may edit, reproduce and incorporate
your comments in Lonely Planet products such as
guidebooks, websites and digital products, so let us
know if you don't want your comments reproduced or
your name acknowledged. For a copy of our privacy
policy visit *lonelyplanet.com/privacy*.

MILES RODDIS

Miles and his wife have lived in Valencia's Barrio del Carmen for nearly 20 years. From here, he sallies forth to write for Lonely Planet, mostly about Mediterranean lands. But nothing is so satisfying as interpreting a place you call home to others and sharing its secrets. Because research is a constant, pleasurable task, he can truly say, hand on paunch, that he's dined in nearly every restaurant that features and drunk in just about every bar.

MILES' THANKS

Thanks, very specially, to Ingrid for her wise insights, smart tip-offs and rigorous proofing. Rosa Ríos gave me some much-appreciated leads on the contemporary art scene in Valencia and Lisa Gingles briefed me on what's what in fashion and shopping. Poppy and Lily cast their experienced clubbing eyes over my drafts and Samantha Hellwege and Jessica Collette described with panache their favourite clubs and pubs. Special thanks too to Jordan Mirchev for his sage advice. Other insights into the club scene came from Christian Pereira, Elena Gómez, plus Robert Dean and his students at the Escuela Oficial de Idiomas, Quart de Poblet. Thanks too to congenial dining companions Carla, Peter, Tim, Diana, Derek and Abu Arturo.

THE PHOTOGRAPHER

Born and raised in Warsaw, Poland, Krzysztof Dydyński discovered pretty early a passion for worldwide travel, which took him on various trips across Europe, Asia and the Americas, and finally to Australia where he now lives. He first visited Valencia more than 30 years ago and regularly returns to Spain. He's witnessed Valencia's spectacular rise from a rather little-known city to a great international travel destination, now almost as famous as its big sisters, Madrid and Barcelona, and a fascinating and ever-changing place for a photographer to work.

Cover photograph Ciudad de las Artes y las Ciencias, Crack Photos Photo Library. **Internal photographs** by Bildarchiv Monheim/GmbH/Alamy p14; Kevin Foy/Alamy p19; Daniel Belenguer/Alamy p117; imagebroker/Alamy p122. All other photographs by Lonely Planet Images, and by Krzysztof Dydyński except Greg Elms p 6 (top), p8-9, p21, p22, p28 (top & bottom), p30, p32, p70, p113; Simon Greenwood p23, p121; Hannah Levy p6 (bottom), p24, p48; Neil Setchfield p128; David Tomlinson p27.

All images are copyright of the photographers unless otherwise indicated. Many of the images in this guide are available for licensing from **Lonely Planet Images:** lonelyplanetimages.com

Palau de les Arts Reina Sofía at the Ciudad de las Artes y las Ciencas (p10)

CONTENTS

THIS IS VALENCIA

Let's put Valencia first. So often compared with the capital, Madrid, or Catalan Barcelona, this lovely city nowadays speaks for herself – yet with a sideways glance at what her big sisters are up to and an occasional thumb of the nose in their direction.

For an increasing number of visitors, Spain's third-largest city is their first choice for a short break. They come to shop in the designer emporia and boutiques, to stroll the historic quarter and to visit the architecturally stunning City of Arts & Sciences complex. And many make sure their program allows time for lazing on Valencia's broad, 3km-long beach, savouring one of the city's more than 300 cloudless days each year. They'll then explore the new marina with its small cluster of chic summertime bars and restaurants, legacy of Valencia's 2007 hosting of the America's Cup sailing races.

   The city is an appealing mix of the traditional and ultramodern, buzzing with a Mediterranean energy. After work on Friday, the same young woman may nibble a tapa or two with friends or dine alfresco on a restaurant terrace, then relax in the vast chill-out zone of Tarraza Umbracle before heading down to the discoteca below. After she's grabbed a few hours sleep, you might spot her on her father's arm at a neighbourhood fiesta, wearing full traditional Fallas regalia, her elaborate, embroidered baroque dress billowing with petticoats. Same girl, same city, same sense of style.

   Yes, Valencia is very much a party town. Las Fallas, Europe's wildest street party, sets the tone in mid-March. But every weekend the nightlife throbs until beyond dawn. Gastronomically too, Valencia has everything from smart restaurants serving haute cuisine to small family concerns offering hearty, economical fare. What they share is the freshest produce, plucked from the *huerta*, the surrounding fertile agricultural plain. And paella, now known the world over, first simmered over a wood fire here in Valencia…

Top Calle de Caballeros (p36), Barrio del Carmen **Bottom** Traditionally dressed women at Las Fallas (p24) celebrations

>HIGHLIGHTS

Valencia Town Hall (p62) on Plaza del Ayuntamiento

>1 CIUDAD DE LAS ARTES Y LAS CIENCIAS

BE DWARFED BY SPACE-AGE SPLENDOUR

A harp, its tip stabbing the sky, a whale skeleton, Darth Vader's helmet and a giant, never blinking eye: your mind will boggle at these images as it struggles to take in the wondrous forms of the City of Arts & Sciences. Bursting out of the old riverbed from what was quite recently rank, untended marshland, it was shaped in the main by internationally renowned architect Santiago Calatrava, the city's most famous contemporary son (see p147).

The filaments of the Assut d'Or reach for the sky like a giant sail – or *jamonero* (ham slicer), as the locals rapidly and less reverently dubbed it. This broad bridge splits the space between the spiky exterior of the Museo de las Ciencias Príncipe Felipe and the Ágora, a giant, multifunctional, recently completed lotus of a structure.

Just downstream is the Oceanogràfic, in whose aquariums sloshes enough water to fill 15 Olympic-size swimming pools.

Upstream, the Hemisfèric, at once IMAX cinema, planetarium and laser show, broods like a huge, heavy-lidded eye over the shallow lake that laps around it. Beyond it, the Palau de les Arts Reina Sofía,

the most imposing structure, its shell shimmering with bright, white *trencadís* (slivers-of-broken-tile mosaic), resembles a supine armadillo. With its four auditoriums and seating for 4400, this opera house defers in size only to Sydney's iconic structure.

Linking the central core is L'Umbracle, a 320m-long walkway shaded by diaphanous, feathery arches that recall the ribs of a palm frond. Of a summer evening, few things are more pleasant than sitting beneath it and sipping a cocktail.

But you're probably here for what's within. Supplementing the high-tech pleasures of the Hemisfèric, the watery world of the Oceanogràfic, Europe's largest aquarium, offers polar zones, a dolphinarium, a Red Sea aquarium and a Mediterranean seascape. There are a couple of underwater tunnels, one 70m long, where the fish, including sharks, giant eels and rays, swim all around you.

Signage within the Museo de las Ciencias Príncipe Felipe is in English as well as Spanish. The innards of this science museum are dwarfed to a degree by the monumental scale of the structure itself, but there are still plenty of touchy-feely things for children, and machines, displays and interactive panels to arouse even the most unscientific of adults.

For opening hours and tariffs, see p98.

>2 PLAZA DE LA VIRGEN

FEEL THE CITY'S HEARTBEAT

Pedestrianised Plaza de la Virgen usually seethes. Children chase pigeons, busy commuters pass through without a glance, while folk with more time linger over a drink on one of the broad cafe terraces. After dark, street performers emerge and the plaza's smooth marble surface is a favourite for skateboarders and rollerbladers. Turn up on Sunday morning and you've a good chance of seeing folk dancing. Arrive just before noon on Thursday and you'll witness the Tribunal de las Aguas (Water Court; p50), Europe's oldest legal institution.

The square has always been busy, ever since the time when it was the forum and focal point of Roman Valencia. You may find it crowded but numbers are nothing compared to the morning of the second Sunday in May. Then, a statuette of the Virgin Mary, who gives her name to the square, makes the journey, all of 200m but lasting more than 20 minutes, from her basilica to the cathedral as passionate crowds surge to touch her robes. On 17 and 18 March, more than 20,000 *falleros* and *falleras* (male and female festival participants) process through the square, bearing bouquets and huge mounted displays of flowers as offerings to Her.

The reclining figure in the gushing fountain represents the Río Turia, retaining his dignity despite the pigeon guano spattered over his handsome form. The eight maidens with their overflowing pots symbolise the main irrigation canals flowing from the river.

In the flamboyant Gothic Capilla del Santo Cáliz, to the right of the main entrance of the cathedral (p48), is what's claimed to be the Holy Grail, the chalice from which Christ sipped during the Last Supper and one of a dozen or more rival claimants. A door leads to the cathedral museum with its rich collection of vestments and statuary. The next chapel along, the Capilla de San Francisco de Borja, has a pair of particularly sensitive Goyas.

The suffused light streams through the translucent alabaster windows of the tower above the main altar. Here too, wonderfully vivid late-15th-century frescoes, concealed beneath stucco for centuries, were revealed during recent restoration.

For superb 360-degree city and skyline views, turn left as you

enter the cathedral and clamber up the 207 spiralling steps of the octagonal Miguelete bell tower (for times, see p48).

Above the altar of the church, or basilica, of 17th-century Nuestra Señora de los Desamparados, is the ornate, much-venerated statue of the Virgin, patron of the city. If you arrive after hours, peer in through the grilles on the southern, cathedral side, and push your nose against its bars, worn smooth over the years by tens of thousands of supplicants.

Opposite, and a symbol of secular power, is the handsome 15th-century Gothic – and much amended – Palau de la Generalitat (p39).

>3 INSTITUTO VALENCIANO DE ARTE MODERNO (IVAM)

SAVOUR WORLD-CLASS CONTEMPORARY ART

IVAM (*ee-bam*) is one of Europe's finest museums of contemporary art. Permanent elements include a whole gallery of spiky, abstract creations in metal by the 20th-century Catalan sculptor Julio Gonzalez and his contemporaries, and another area devoted to Ignacio Pinazo, the late-19th-century Valencian artist. The museum also holds a copious collection of photography from its earliest days until now, elements of which are often on display.

Most visitors come to enjoy the museum's temporary exhibitions, hugely varied, of a consistently high standard and always illustrated on IVAM's website, so you can cherry pick in advance.

Mixing the strictly contemporary with the past, there's a hefty length of the old city wall in the Sala de la Muralla, a gallery beneath the museum that's devoted to temporary exhibitions. Also well worth a visit is IVAM's bookshop. It carries much more than books and is a good place to find stylish gifts for the folks back home.

For more details, see p38.

>4 MERCADO CENTRAL

PICK YOUR WAY ROUND EUROPE'S LARGEST FRESH PRODUCE MARKET

There's been a market on this very spot since medieval times. Facing the Gothic splendour of La Lonja across Plaza del Mercado, today's wonderful Modernista building is a swirl of smells, movement and colour. Here are more than 900 active stalls, despite ever keener competition from supermarkets. Look among all this activity for the few remaining single-product stalls offering, only and exclusively, snails by the sackful, or multicoloured spices that contrast with the monochrome green of bean or lettuce stalls and the bright orange and lemon of the citrus vendors.

In the annexe on its northern side, you'll find shoals of seafood and fish. Eels too, freshly hauled from the Albufera Lake (p119) and still slithering. Squirm in turn at the pair of counters in one corner that specialise in whole sheep's heads, lungs, tongues, trotters, tripe and other offal.

Don't forget to look at the structure itself, recently scrubbed and polished anew: the way the light pours in (despite the netting protecting you from pigeon droppings), the glowing coloured glass and the mosaics on the facade. For opening times, see p50.

house of the America's CUP
casa de la

> 5 THE INNER PORT
FEEL THE SEA BREEZE AT A SLEEK LEISURE HARBOUR

What draws *valencianos* here by the hundreds on warm weekends and summer nights is the cluster of new restaurants, clubs and bars that snuggle around the landmark Veles e Vents building (p92) and out along the promontory leading to the Marina Real Juan Carlos I, with its moorings for 43 luxury yachts and around 1500 more modest craft. Walk to the end of the jetty, let the breeze ruffle your hair, and look back at the curve of the harbour. Then, for a unique perspective of this new development, take a catamaran cruise (p92), ideally at sunset.

Nowadays, the bright glass cubes, one for each of the 2007 America's Cup teams, ring the horseshoe-shaped inner harbour. At its heart, the original, Italianate port building with its imposing clock tower still stands proud among the ultramodern.

The America's Cup was a catalyst for the wholesale redevelopment of Valencia's port. The busy commercial area, Spain's third largest, is now banished beyond the slim barrier of a canal constructed especially for the yachting jamboree. From the wharves leave 20% of the country's exports – everything from crates of plump oranges to Ford cars by the thousand, assembled at the multinational's factory south of town. Exiled too, just to the south, are the former fishing port and ferry terminal for the Balearic Islands.

>6 BIOPARC

EXPERIENCE AN ECOFRIENDLY ANIMAL PARK, VALENCIA'S NEWEST ATTRACTION

'Zoo' is far too old-fashioned and inapt a term for this innovative, ecofriendly and gently educational space. Six years in gestation and costing €60 million, it let the public loose on its animals for the first time in 2008.

The whole space is landscaped so that the eye simply doesn't perceive fences and barriers – just the sweep of the savannah (the main habitat) where elephants wander among simulated baobab trees and the lion lies down with the giraffe, warthog or wildebeest. Progress to the dense foliage of the Equatorial Africa section. Then explore Madagascar, where large-eyed lemurs gambol around your ankles without fear. All the animals roaming freely in this section are endangered species in their natural habitat.

In the thatched restaurant, grab a waterside table and watch the wildlife just beyond your reach as you sip a drink or tuck into lunch to the rhythms of African music.

For times and tariffs, see p106.

>7 LA LONJA

WONDER AT A GORGEOUS GOTHIC CHAMBER OF COMMERCE

The clean, sweeping lines of Gothic La Lonja are the perfect antidote if you're feeling a twinge of indigestion at so much rich baroque around town. This Unesco World Heritage site, constructed in the early 16th century, was at once commodity exchange, elementary bank and meeting place for the merchant classes. The Sala de Contratación, the main colonnaded hall, gives onto a little courtyard garden with a fine external staircase that ascends to the Consulado del Mar.

Soaring, slim, twisted pillars, curling high like sticks of barley sugar, support the rib-vaulted ceiling of the Sala de Contratación. They invite architectural metaphor: fashioned to resemble skeins of silk, some say, while others think they're crafted to suggest the ropes and hawsers of the merchant ships that brought and exported the city's wealth. Up high in a salutary message (still relevant today), the encircling band of Latin writing avers that in a good business deal 'there is no lie in the speech, no deceit and no lending money with interest… The merchant who acts thus will prosper plentifully and enjoy eternal life.'

Across the courtyard, a stunning coffered ceiling looks down upon the 1st-floor Consulado del Mar, while outside each Sunday stamp and coin collectors exchange and trade, sustaining in their modest, part-time way the building's original function. For opening hours, see p49.

V

>8 OLD TURIA RIVERBED

WALK, RIDE OR SKATE A 9KM GREEN SNAKE

No visit to Valencia is complete without a walk, jog, bike or skate through at least part of the Jardines del Turia, a 9km-long lung of green. It's a glorious mix of playing fields, cycling and walking paths, trees, fountains, lawns and children's playgrounds (notably the magnificent reclining, ever-patient giant, Gulliver; p98).

Two unmissable Valencia sights plug each end of the green, one-time bed of the Río Turia. At its eastern limit rear the multiple attractions of the City of Arts & Sciences (p10), each one a monumental architectural temple to human achievement. At the western extremity, the environmentally aware Bioparc (p17) subtly and altogether more gently recreates the natural habitats of its animal residents.

As you savour this unique space at the heart of a big city, it's hard to believe that, when the course of the Río Turia was diverted after the disastrous floods of 1957, one serious proposal was to drive a motorway along its original length. Fortunately, this superficially seductive idea, taking advantage of a ready-made thoroughfare to the port, was rejected. After years of languishing and piecemeal development, the whole length is now landscaped and plans are in hand to tame the last sour, wild stretch that leads to the Mediterranean.

>9 MUSEO DE BELLAS ARTES

ENJOY CLASSIC CANVASES IN SPAIN'S SECOND-LARGEST FINE ARTS MUSEUM

Once a fusty, ill-lit place, Valencia's Fine Arts Museum is nowadays bright, spacious, well lit and worthy of its splendid collection. The ground floor houses mainly religious art, confiscated in 1837 (like the basis of so many Spanish museum collections) when the state seized ecclesiastical properties. Highlights include several magnificent late medieval altarpieces (especially the *Retablo del Fray Bonifacio Ferrer*). On the 1st floor are works by greats such as El Greco, Murillo, Morales, Goya and a swashbuckling Velázquez self-portrait. The museum is also well endowed with canvases from Valencia's first golden age of painting, with works by internationally recognised artists such as Ribera, Ribalta and Juan de Juanes. On this floor too is a magnificent Roman *Mosaic of the Nine Muses*. Up on the 2nd floor, galleries feature the Valencian impressionist school and its leading exponents, Sorolla and Pinazo.

Back on the ground floor (turn left into the gallery just before the main exit) there's a quirky canvas of Cristo del Salvador (Christ the Saviour) floating past the Torres Serranos, the work of the 17th-century artist Vicente Salvador Gómez.

Galleries aren't numbered but the floor plan, in English, will guide you to a degree.

See p99 for more.

>10 A SEASIDE PAELLA

SAMPLE PAELLA WHERE IT FIRST SIMMERED

Paella, *valencianos* proudly claim, first simmered and bubbled here beside the Mediterranean. And at weekends locals in their hundreds head for Las Arenas and the long line of simple rice and seafood restaurants that run beside the promenade. Join them for an experience that, for many, amounts almost to a pilgrimage.

The finished paella will be flourished for your approbation. A *sotto voce* 'mm', even discreet applause, will be well received as your waiter asks if you wish to eat convivially and communally from the pan or have it spooned out on plates.

One more point of etiquette; paella is only eaten – by the tonne, all over town, ordered by the panful or as a *ración*, a single serving -- at lunchtime. If it's on a restaurant's dinner menu, you've chosen one that knows its tourist trade.

See p92 for places to eat.

>11 ESTACIÓN DEL NORTE

STAND WITHIN A MODERNISTA MARVEL AND TRANSPORT HUB

The best way to reach Valencia is by train – not for the journey, but for arriving here. You'll be one of the 90,000-plus passengers who each day bustle through the station's majestic main hall, its dark, stained wood relieved by shimmering *trencadís*.

Like many of the great railway terminals of Europe, it was built to impress, to implant in the visitor a first, positive impression of the city. The exterior seems a cross between a mock castle and a rich, creamy wedding cake. The whole is a gorgeous example of Valencian Modernismo, rich in decorative touches that enhance what is in essence a functional place for mass transportation.

Illustrating Valencia's industry and the *huerta*, the city's surrounding fertile agricultural plain, the decoration (cheery peasant women in traditional costume with naked, frolicking children at their skirts, baskets brimming with fruit and friezes of oranges) is lovely for its own sake – even if some contemporary *valencianos* do squirm at the clichéd themes. See p74 for more.

>VALENCIA DIARY

Noise and light are the essential ingredients of many a Spanish fiesta. Here in Valencia, the volume is turned up louder, the light more intense. *Valencianos* fête a good *pirotécnico*, an artist in fire and explosion, as much as any star bullfighter, and *castillos* (aerial fireworks displays), together with *mascletàs* (a cacophony of eardrum-shattering explosions), accompany most major festivals. The city marks its major religious days – the unique Corpus Cristi celebrations, Holy Week and celebrations in honour of its pair of San Vicentes – less exuberantly but equally colourfully.

Men with fresh ammunition at La Tomatina festival (p121)

JANUARY

Fiesta de San Vicente Mártir

Every 22 January the city celebrates the day of its patron saint, the 3rd-century martyr San Vicente.

FEBRUARY

Valencia Escena Oberta

www.festivalveo.com, in Spanish
Valencia Open Stage offers 10 days of Spanish and European street theatre, dance and startling contemporary art.

MARCH TO APRIL

Las Fallas

Five frenetic days of outdoor action in Europe's largest street party. Round-the-clock festivities include street parties, paella-cooking competitions, parades, open-air concerts, bullfights and nightly free fireworks displays. See p130.

Semana Santa Marinera

Elaborate Easter Holy Week processions in the maritime district of Malvarrosa. For a flavour of the processions, visit Casa-Museo de la Semana Santa Marinera (p90).

Ninots (near-life-sized figurines that strut and pose) near Estación del Norte (p74) during Las Fallas

Corpus Christi celebrations

Fiesta de San Vicente Ferrer

On the Sunday following Easter, a parade of town worthies honours Valencia's other and equally venerated San Vicente, while playlets recount his miracles.

MAY

Danza Valencia

Strictly contemporary dancing by Spanish and international troupes during two weeks spanning late April and early May.

Fiesta de la Virgen

On the second Sunday of May, the effigy of the Virgen de los Desamparados, hemmed in by fervent believers struggling to touch her, makes the short journey across Plaza de la Virgen to the cathedral. See p12.

JUNE

Corpus Christi

Biblical, apocryphal and fantastic characters parade, and children perform mystery plays aboard the giant carts of Las Rocas (see p39).

Día de San Juan

On 24 June, *valencianos* by the thousand mark the year's shortest night with bonfires on the beaches.

JULY

Feria de Julio

www.feriadejulio.com, in Spanish

In the second half of July, this festival features performing arts, brass-band competitions, bullfights and fireworks, culminating in a magnificent 'battle of the flowers'.

OCTOBER TO NOVEMBER

Día de la Comunidad

Each 9 October Valencia celebrates its 1238 liberation from the Arabs with processions and elaborate Moros y Cristianos (Moors and Christians) parades.

Mostra de Valencia

A week for film buffs, celebrating cinema from all around the Mediterranean.

Valencia Bienal

www.bienaldevalencia.com

Held over two months in odd-numbered years, the Valencia Bienal festival of visual art showcases works from around 50 Spanish and international contemporary creators.

>ITINERARIES

A predator approaches an underwater tunnel at the Oceanogràfic (p11)

ITINERARIES

The active heart of Valencia is so compact that you can spend your time visiting rather than travelling. The city merits a good week of your life but few visitors can afford such indulgence. Here we list three full days of activity plus suggestions for shopaholics, the best in dining and ways to stretch your euros.

DAY ONE

The City of Arts & Sciences (p10) will take you a full day to explore. Within it, the Oceanogràfic is a must-see; the most original of its several eating options is Restaurante Submarino (p100). Rest your weary feet by taking in an Imax film at the Hemisfèric. Should you be game for more, head into town to visit, according to your artistic preference, the Museo de Bellas Artes (p20) or the Instituto Valenciano de Arte Moderno (p14).

DAY TWO

Begin by browsing Mercado Central (p15), then cross the road to explore La Lonja (p18). Visit the cathedral and church of Nuestra Señora de los Desamparados (p12). Allow a full afternoon to explore Bioparc (p17), open until dusk and a splendid Valencia attraction. In fact plan to eat there – especially if you have children – at its splendid, economical bush house restaurant with the animals so near they could almost snatch your sandwiches.

DAY THREE

Take the bus or high-speed tram for a seaside morning, exploring the old port (p16), walking the *paseo marítimo* (the promenade), and perhaps relaxing on the beach and enjoying a swim. For lunch, order a paella at one of Las Arenas' beachside restaurants (p92).

In the afternoon, take bus 95 and visit Museo de Historia de Valencia (p107) at the city's western extremity. Time it right and you can climb the small hillock in adjacent Parque de Cabecera (p108) to watch the sun set over town.

Top The magnificent rib-vaulted interior of La Lonja (p18) **Bottom** A prickly landscape at Jardín Botánico (p106)

ITINERARIES

VALENCIA FOR FREE

On Sunday, many museums and sights don't charge (see p80). Any day of the week is fine for sprawling on the beach (free showers too) or exploring Valencia on foot: see p113 for three suggested walking routes. The Centro Histórico is fun to browse, with or without a map in your hand, while the *cauce,* Valencia's former riverbed, is a great stretch for traffic-free strolling. And a couple of near-freebies: for €1, relax in the shady confines of the Jardín Botánico (p106). Or sip a coffee, lasting as long as you like, on Plaza de la Virgen (p12) or at a promenade cafe overlooking the beach.

SHOP AROUND

Even the most confirmed shopaholic wearies of a solid day of window browsing, so dip in and out of this one. In the Centro Histórico, streets behind La Lonja have modish, hip boutiques (see p51). Break the session with a coffee on the terrace of Café Lisboa (p58). C de Colón, flanked by independent and Spanish chain clothing shops, is the city's main shopping street (see p64). Nearby, tranquil Café de La Nau (p71) is a good spot to escape the scrum. For Valencia's most exclusive shopping, explore the

Shop till you drop at fashion boutiques along C de Colón (p64)

FORWARD PLANNING

For most activities it's fine to do as the *valencianos* do and plan at the last minute. This said, a little advance preparation can save a lot of frustration.

Once you've decided to come Budget airfares rise as departure time approaches, so reserve as far in advance as possible.

Other advance action To avoid possible queues (particularly for the Oceanogràfic), reserve online for the City of Arts & Sciences (www.cac.es). Tickets for the Palau de les Arts often sell out, so book via its website, www.lesarts.com (warning: it's not user-friendly). Bioparc's website (www.bioparcvalencia.es) is only in Spanish; to book, click on *compra de entradas* and the rest is more or less intuitive. Although motor-racing fans can't reserve via www.valenciastreetcircuit.com for the annual Grand Prix of Europe Formula One, the site gives details of where to get tickets. You can book a seat for Valencia Club de Fútbol games at www.servicaixa.com, but it's easier to drop by the shop (p67) once you're in town. The club's www.valenciacf.com gives details of upcoming games and seats still available.

British-run www.thisisvalencia.com has its finger on the pulse of what's on in town, while the official tourist office site (www.turisvalencia.es) is a great source of information.

cluster of streets between C de Colón and Mercado de Colón (see p74), where you can unwind at one of the smart terrace cafes.

A GASTRONOMIC JOURNEY

This one's a blowout so you may prefer to pick at things rather than digest it all at once. Begin with a fishy midday snack at Tasca Ángel (p58), supreme for grilled sardines, or Bar Pilar (p55), *the* place for mussels. Lunchtime *menús del día,* fixed price and normally offering three courses, are a particular bargain. Stay in the Centro Histórico (for ideas, see p40, p55 and p68) or head to L'Eixample (p78). Late afternoon, linger over an *horchata,* this very Valencia drink, on Plaza de Santa Catalina (p59). For dinner you deserve a treat, so indulge in gourmet delights at Michelin one-star restaurants La Sucursal (p42), Riff (p81) or Vertical (p101).

The imposing Torres de Serranos (p40) stands over Plaza de los Fueros

NEIGHBOURHOODS

Though few cities can have changed so radically in the last two decades, exploring Valencia means following the city's expansion over 2000 years.

The city's kernel is the Centro Histórico and, within it, the Barrio del Carmen. Here it all began in 138 BC, when pensioned-off Roman legionnaires established the small settlement they named 'Valentia' on the banks of Río Turia. The town wall that the Arabs built protected the city for centuries. But with the Arabs ousted and Valencia growing, the Christians constructed their own more extensive defensive wall. Today, its only legacies are the massive Torres de Serranos and Torres de Quart, yet its outline still demarcates the Centro Histórico (hop on the No 5 bus and you can beat the bounds of the old city on a 20-minute ride).

The walls were torn down in the mid-19th century as industrialisation brought massive expansion in all directions. The smart bourgeois residences of L'Eixample rose cheek by jowl with the working-class area of Russafa, for centuries a separate village with roots back in Muslim times. Contemporary L'Eixample, with some of Valencia's most elegant shops, retains its sense of exclusiveness yet also has some of the city's most tempting restaurants and bars. Russafa too keeps its popular character – nowadays, it's the city's prime immigrant area – blending into the mix stylish bars, earthy drinking holes and smart eating options.

Throughout their history, *valencianos,* like so many residents of Spanish coastal towns, had lived inland for fear of seaborne attack. But as the city became richer, the port expanded (notably exporting oranges and tangerines by the tonne to the UK) while on days off, the townspeople would escape the city to enjoy the sandy beaches to the north and south. The beach and *paseo marítimo* promenade (together with its popular restaurants) are still the city's greatest summertime escape.

Valencia's most recent spectacular growth pulls the axis of the city eastwards as the City of Arts & Sciences gives impetus to massive housing developments overlooking the former riverbed. This 9km-long course of Río Turia (its flow now diverted southwards) pushes east to west through the town. What other city can boast such a long, green ecofriendly stripe reserved for walkers, cyclists and sportspeople?

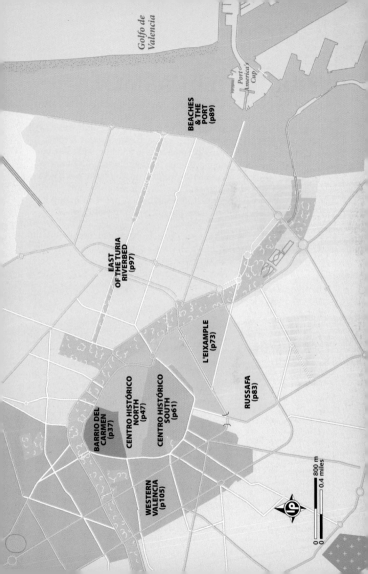

Golfo de Valencia

Port America's Cup

BEACHES & THE PORT (p89)

EAST OF THE TURIA RIVERBED (p97)

L'EIXAMPLE (p73)

RUSSAFA (p83)

BARRIO DEL CARMEN (p37)

CENTRO HISTÓRICO NORTH (p47)

CENTRO HISTÓRICO SOUTH (p61)

WESTERN VALENCIA (p105)

800 m
0.4 miles

0

>BARRIO DEL CARMEN

There are two Carmens: the daytime girl with her boutique clothing stores, museums, galleries and restaurants, and her after-dark sister, frequenter of clubs and cafe terraces, primed for a long night out.

C de Caballeros, the town's main street in medieval times, is sober enough by day. But return around midnight to find bars and cafes, unnoticed in the sunshine, that have flung up their shutters for business.

A couple of decades ago, Valencia's oldest quarter really was a tired old lady. Nowadays, thanks to generous local government grants, long-neglected houses have been restored and public spaces reclaimed. It's not all fun and frolic, though; there are still plenty of empty lots and tottering dwellings.

La Carmé, as she's known in *valenciano,* blends imperceptibly into the rest of the Centro Histórico, of which she's a part. Day or night, the only way to seek out her riches is on foot.

BARRIO DEL CARMEN

⊙ SEE
Casa-Museo José
  Benlliure **1** D1
Iglesia del Carmen **2** D2
Instituto Valenciano de
  Arte Moderno (IVAM) ...**3** B1
La Beneficencia ....(see 5)
Museo de los Soldaditos
  de Plomo **4** D3
Museo de Prehistoria &
  Museo de Etnología **5** B2
Museo del Corpus **6** E2
Palau de la Generalitat ..**7** E3
Plaza del Carmen **8** D2
Torres de Quart **9** A4
Torres de Serranos **10** E2

⌂ SHOP
Bombonerías Nuatté ...**11** E3
Dirty Shirt ....(see 25)
Envinarte **12** E3

⑂ EAT
Ca'an Bermell **13** C2
La Carmé **14** C3
La Huerta La Botella ...**15** D3
La Lluna **16** B2
La Sucursal **17** B2
La Tastaolletes **18** C1
L'Hamadríada **19** C3
Mattilda **20** D2
Orient Xpress **21** E2
Pati Pineda **22** D2

Pepita Pulgarcita **23** E3
Tacita de Plata **24** D1

▼ DRINK
Carmentown **25** C3
Chill Out **26** D3
Jimmy Glass **27** D3
Johnny Maracas **28** D3
L'Ermità ....(see 15)
Sant Jaume **29** C4

★ PLAY
Music Box **30** B3
Turmix **31** C2
Venial **32** C4

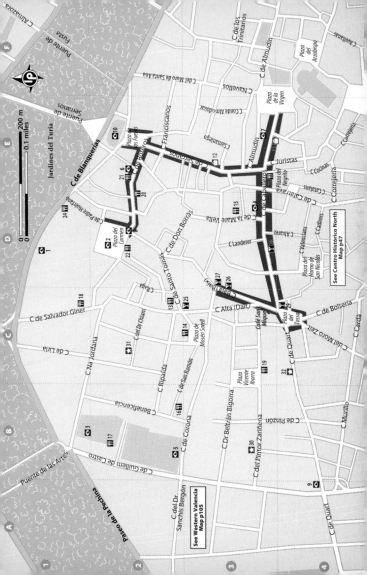

BARRIO DEL CARMEN

◉ SEE

◉ CASA-MUSEO JOSÉ BENLLIURE

☎ 96 391 16 62; C de Blanquerías 23; €2; ⏱ 10am-2pm & 4.30-8.30pm Tue-Sat, 10am-3pm Sun; 🚍 5

This lovely 19th-century bourgeois villa was the home of Valencian artist José Benlliure (1855–1937). Furnished in period style, it's also a gallery dedicated to him and his contemporaries. Beyond the mature rear garden is his agreeably cluttered studio and library.

◉ INSTITUTO VALENCIANO DE ARTE MODERNO (IVAM)

☎ 96 386 30 00; www.ivam.es; C de Guillem de Castro 118; €2; ⏱ 10am-8/10pm Tue-Sun; 🚍 5

Valencia's world standard contemporary art gallery. Free guided tours noon Saturday and 11am Sunday. For more detail, see p14.

◉ MUSEO DE LOS SOLDADITOS DE PLOMO

☎ 96 391 86 75; www.museoliber.org, in Spanish; C de Caballeros 20-22; €4; ⏱ 11am-2pm & 4-7pm Wed-Fri, 10am-3pm & 4-7pm Sat & Sun; 🚍 5, 5b

This delight for boys and men alike claims to hold over a million pieces, making it the world's largest collection of toy soldiers. The vast 4.7m x 2.8m set piece of the Battle of Almansa (1707) has more

Museo de los Soldaditos de Plomo

than 9000 combatants, and cases teem with rank upon rank, battalion following battalion, of toy soldiers, each set resembling so many computer-generated clones.

◉ MUSEO DE PREHISTORIA & MUSEO DE ETNOLOGÍA

☎ 96 388 35 65; C de Corona 36; admission free; ⏱ 10am-8pm Tue-Sun; 🚍 5

This cultural complex, commonly known as La Beneficencia, houses two museums. Highlights include rich finds from the Palaeolithic Cueva de Parpalló and the Guerrero de Moixent, a dinky 4th-century BC miniature plumed warrior on horseback. The Ethnology Museum displays photographs and

NEIGHBOURHOODS

BARRIO DEL CARMEN

household items from the city's recent past.

◎ MUSEO DEL CORPUS

☎ 96 315 31 56; C de Roteros 3; admission free; ☉ 10am-2pm & 4.30-8.30pm Tue-Sat, 10am-3pm Sun; 🚌 5

Behind tall doors rest Las Rocas, giant carts that are wheeled out to celebrate Valencia's June Corpus Cristi festival. Their paintwork darkened with age, the earliest dates back to the 16th century. Upstairs are displayed the fanciful costumes and props that feature in the Corpus Cristi procession.

◎ PALAU DE LA GENERALITAT

☎ 96 318 44 30; C de Caballeros 2; 🚌 5, 5b

The handsome 15th-century Palau de la Generalitat is the seat of government for the Valencia region. Its symmetry is recent; the renaissance tower – the one facing Plaza de la Virgen – had

to wait more than 400 years for its perfectly matching partner, erected in 1951.

◎ PLAZA DEL CARMEN

🚌 5

The freshly scrubbed 17th-century baroque facade of the Iglesia del Carmen looms over this pleasant, traffic-free square. Within, there's little of interest but for one illuminating detail from recent Spanish history: a portly Generalísimo Franco kneels, left, among the saints in the huge wall painting behind the altar. Opposite the church is the less flamboyant but equally satisfying frontage of the 18th-century Palacio de Pineda.

◎ TORRES DE QUART

C de Guillem de Castro; admission free; ☉ 10am-2pm & 4.30-8.30pm Tue-Sat, 10am-3pm Sun; 🚌 5

You can climb to the top of these twin 15th-century towers. Serving

---

THE CORPUS CHRISTI PROCESSION

Stand among the spectators every ninth Sunday after Easter and you're witnessing an enactment that was first performed in 1355. The procession portrays in spectacle and dance personages from the Old and New Testaments. Processing too are several apocryphal characters who bear only the most tenuous links to Christianity. Over the centuries, the tradition has been much modified. Characters too have changed. Beside Gigantes, four pairs of giant figures representing the four continents (Australia had still to be discovered when they were first paraded in the 16th century), walk and wobble a Valencian couple in contemporary dress. And everyone keeps an eye open for La Moma, representing Virtue and veiled in white from head to toe. Portrayed by a man, she resists the seven stick-wielding deadly sins who prowl around her.

NEIGHBOURHOODS

BARRIO DEL CARMEN

for centuries as a prison, they were originally designed to resemble those of the Castel Nuovo in Naples (which at the time belonged to Spain). Up high, you can still see the pockmarks caused by French cannonballs when Napoleonic troops invaded the city in 1808.

🔘 TORRES DE SERRANOS
Plaza de los Fueros; €2; 🕑 10am-2pm & 4.30-8.30pm Tue-Sat, 10am-3pm Sun; 🚌 5
The well-preserved, 14th-century Torres de Serranos, scrubbed and softly illuminated at night, over-look the bed of Río Turia. Climb its 132 steps to the battlements for an impressive panoramic view of the old quarter – it requires less effort than the longer slog up the stairs of the Miguelete bell tower (p12).

🛍 SHOP
🏷 BOMBONERÍAS NUATTÉ
Chocolate & Sweets
☎ 96 391 37 91; C de Caballeros 7; 🕑 10am-2pm & 5-8.30pm Mon-Sat, 11.30am-2pm Sun; 🚌 5, 5b
This little shop specialises in top quality chocolates. For an original take-home present, if you can keep your fingers off them, buy a box of the round chocs embossed – also in chocolate – with the city's major monuments.

🏷 DIRTY SHIRT *Fashion*
☎ 96 391 56 48; C Alta 32; 🕑 11am-2pm & 5-9pm Tue-Sat; 🚌 5
You could almost be in downtown Chicago. Drop in for the latest in street-cred sweatshirts, hoodies, sneakers (the pair that is slowly revolving on the counter will mesmerise you into releasing your grip on your credit card), sports- and beachwear.

🏷 ENVINARTE
Wines, Gifts & Souvenirs
☎ 96 391 39 30; www.envinarte.es, in Spanish; C de Serranos 6; 🕑 10.30am-2.30pm & 5.30-9pm Tue-Sat; 🚌 5, 5b
Teresa Almeida, fluent in English and a qualified sommelier, chooses her wines with knowledge and flair and carries a particularly inviting selection of Spanish vintages. Next door but one, Envinarte Fusión, her more recent creation, is a minor feast of tasteful gifts to take home.

🍴 EAT
🍴 CA'AN BERMELL *Tapas*　€€
☎ 96 391 02 88; C de Santo Tomás 18; 🕑 lunch & dinner Tue-Sat, dinner Mon; 🚌 5
Baleful-eyed fish and tumbling seafood packed in ice fill Ca'an Bermell's window. This long-established restaurant with its sim-ple wooden tables and benches serves the freshest of tapas.

Teresa Almeida
Sommelier and wine- and gift-shop owner

Qualified sommelier twice over and wine-shop owner. How come? I've always loved the world of wine – how it's produced, the gastronomy that goes with it, everything. I spent 13 years in the restaurant business, seven of them responsible for the wine lists. **Anywhere I might know?** I served my time in Bodega Casa Montaña (p92), for example, and more recently with Seu-Xerea (p57). **Why the Barrio del Carmen?** Hombre, there's nowhere more *valenciano*. And I lived and worked here for many years. **Where do you go for a good night out?** I love unwinding at Terraza Umbracle (p103) or on the terrace of Café-Bar Negrito (p58). For dancing and chilling out, it has to be Las Ánimas Puerto (p95). **And for a meal?** I love the informality and great food of La Torrija (p86).

In season, it offers all kinds of mushrooms and dishes seasoned with wild truffles.

🍴 LA CARMÉ *Mediterranean* €€

☎ 96 392 25 32; Plaza de Mosén Sorell; ☽ dinner Mon-Sat; 🚍 5, 5b

The *menú* at La Carmé – things are kept simple and it only does a set meal (€21) – has scarcely changed in two decades. Why should it when, with its pleasing decor of wood and bare brick and its friendly service, the place offers such superb value?

🍴 LA HUERTA LA BOTELLA

International €€

☎ 96 392 37 05; C del Obispo Don Jerónimo 8; ☽ lunch & dinner Tue-Fri, dinner Sat; 🚍 5, 5b

Down a little-walked side street parallel to C de Caballeros, this bright newcomer offers cuisine that's as innovative as its striking design, where original artwork on the walls competes with a giant blowup of the Centro Histórico. Its lunchtime *menú* (€15) offers exceptional value.

🍴 LA LLUNA *Vegetarian* €

☎ 96 392 21 46; C de San Ramón 23; ☽ lunch & dinner Mon-Sat; 🚍 5; Ⓥ

Friendly and full of regulars, with walls of clashing tilework and the kitchen on full view, well-established La Lluna serves qual-

ity, reasonably priced vegetarian fare. On two floors (smoking upstairs, smoke-free below – the compromise works well), it offers lots of choices, including an outstanding value four-course lunch *menú* (€7) that changes daily.

🍴 LA SUCURSAL

Mediterranean Fusion €€€

☎ 96 374 66 65; www.restaurantela sucursal.com, in Spanish; C de Guillem de Castro 118; ☽ lunch & dinner Mon-Fri, dinner Sat; 🚍 5

La Sucursal, restaurant of IVAM (p14), is appropriately contemporary, all muted greys and blacks, subtly illuminated. At this Michelin one-star restaurant, fish is the freshest and the wine list is a veritable book (abstainers can choose from more than 30 different mineral waters!). The *menú degustación* (€68) is a sheer delight to linger over.

🍴 LA TASTAOLLETES

Vegetarian, Spanish €€

☎ 96 392 18 62; C de Salvador Giner 6; ☽ dinner Mon-Sat, lunch Tue-Sat; 🚍 5; Ⓥ

This tiny place does a creative range of vegetarian tapas and mains. Pleasantly informal, its star attributes are the friendly atmosphere and good, wholesome food created from quality prime ingredients. Salads are frondy and all sauces and desserts (indulge in the cheesecake with stewed fruits) are homemade.

🍴 L'HAMADRÍADA

Mediterranean Fusion €€

☎ 96 326 08 91; www.hamadriada .com, in Spanish; Plaza Vicente Iborra 3; ⏱ lunch Sun-Tue, lunch & dinner Wed-Sat; 🚍 5, 5b

Staff are well-informed and attentive at the Wood Nymph, where everybody seems to know everyone else. Down a short, blind alley, this slim white rectangle of a place does an innovative midday *menú* (€10), perfectly simmered rice dishes and grills where the meat, like the vegetables, is of prime quality.

🍴 MATTILDA *Spanish* €€

☎ 96 382 31 68; C de Roteros 21; ⏱ lunch & dinner Mon-Sat; 🚍 5

The decor is stylish, modern and unpretentious, just like Francisco Borell and his cheery young team, who offer friendly service, an imaginative à la carte selection (including the best Argentinean beef and the restaurant's own foie gras, made on the premises) and a particularly good-value lunch *menú* (€11).

🍴 ORIENT XPRESS

Asian €

☎ 96 306 51 16; www.orientxpress.info; C de Roteros 12; ⏱ noon-midnight Wed-Mon; 🚍 5

Valencia's original noodle bar, where you sit at long wooden tables, offers reasonably priced Japanese, Thai and Malay specialities and great fruit juices. Especially handy if you want to eat outside normal restaurant hours, it also has plenty of vegetarian options.

🍴 PATI PINEDA

Mediterranean Fusion €

☎ 96 391 22 62; Plaza del Carmen 4; ⏱ lunch Mon-Fri Sep-Jul; 🚍 5

Within the Palacio Pineda (these days university premises), this cooperative offers a superb-value creative lunchtime *menú* (€10) that's a favourite with discerning *valencianos*. It's open to all; go through the main door and head for the lone palm tree that shades the rear patio. Do reserve.

🍴 PEPITA PULGARCITA

Tapas €€

☎ 96 391 46 08; C de Caballeros 19; ⏱ 1pm-1.30am Tue-Sun, 7pm-1.30am Mon; 🚍 5, 5b

With wines stacked high behind the bar, and subtle, inventive tapas, tastefully presented, tiny Pepita Pulgarcita is great for a snack, meal or simply a *copa*. The menu is the same down to the last toothpick at **Espita Gorgorita** (☎ 96 392 58 35; Plaza de San Jaime 3; ⏱ noon-midnight), its younger sister just along the street.

🍴 TACITA DE PLATA
Mediterranean, Tapas €€
☎ 96 391 11 06; www.tacitadeplata
.es; cnr C de Blanquerías & Padre
Huérfano; 🕑 lunch & dinner Mon-Fri,
dinner Sat; 🚌 5
Chic Tacita de Plata is a relative
newcomer. Savour its strictly contemporary decor, pleasant, open
atmosphere and reliable Spanish
cuisine, whether you're here to
pick at tapas or enjoy a full meal.

🍸 DRINK
🍸 CARMENTOWN *Music Bar*
☎ 615 98 98 89; C Alta 28; 🕑 7pm-
1.30am Mon-Sat; 🚌 5
Clad in black and white, Carmentown is for connoisseurs of the very
best in black music. Professional DJ
Xino, the genial owner, picks from
his personal, eclectic collection. Curl
up the spiral staircase to its more
intimate, if smokier, upper level or
enjoy its small rear terrace.

🍸 CHILL OUT *Cocktail Bar*
☎ 663 53 95 44; C Baja 20; 🕑 6pm-
1.30am; 🚌 5, 5b
Sink into soft cushions and call
up a mojito, speciality of Markos,
the friendly Croatian barman, or
another of his wicked cocktails.
Chill Out is just that – a place
to relax, down at floor level, as
candles flicker and coloured lights
softly mutate.

🍸 JIMMY GLASS *Music Bar*
www.jimmyglassjazz.net, in Spanish; C
Baja 28; 🕑 8pm-2.30am Sun-Thu, 8pm-
3.30am Fri & Sat; 🚌 5, 5b
It's exclusively jazz at Jimmy Glass,
its walls clad with photos of giants
of the genre. It's just what a jazz bar
should be – dim, smoky and serving
jumbo measures of cocktails. The
owner plays the coolest of sounds
from his vast CD collection and
there's a live combo every other
Tuesday at 9.30pm.

🍸 JOHNNY MARACAS
Cocktail Bar
☎ 96 391 52 66; C de Caballeros 39;
🕑 7pm-3.30am; 🚌 5, 5b
For seriously hip Latino, smart,
bamboo-clad Johnny Maracas is
your bar. Monday to Wednesday,
it's live *batucada* and *capoeira*
from Brazil, Thursday to Saturday is for slinky salsa with a very
Cuban flavour, while Sunday is
Argentinean night.

🍸 L'ERMITÀ *Bar, Cafe*
☎ 96 391 67 59; C del Obispo Don
Jerónimo 4; 🕑 6pm-1.30am Tue-Sun;
🚌 5, 5b
Local English-language graduate
Lucia and her Chilean partner run
this friendly, arty, L-shaped bar
with its walls of mellow brick and
chunky stone. Musical instruments
dangle from the ceiling and art
exhibitions change regularly.

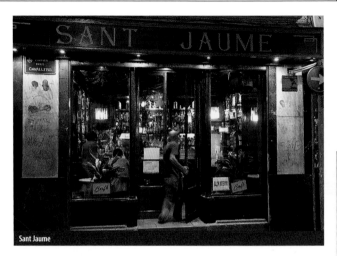

Sant Jaume

⟨Y⟩ SANT JAUME *Bar, Cafe*
☎ 96 391 24 01; C de Caballeros 51;
🕐 noon-midnight; 🚌 5, 5b
The lovely wooden bar was once
the counter of this converted
pharmacy. There's no room to
drink at it but ample space on the
outside terrace, ideal for people-
watching. Alternatively, the 1st
floor is all intimate crannies and
quaint, poky passageways.

★ PLAY
★ MUSIC BOX *Club*
☎ 96 391 41 51; C del Pintor Zariñena
16; 🕐 midnight-7am Tue-Sat; 🚌 5
This sibling of Radio City (p59),
recently restyled and renamed,

beats until dawn. The DJs pride
themselves on their eclectic,
selections which have something
to suit everyone. Entry to the club
is free except after 3am on Friday
and Saturday, when there is a €10
cover charge.

★ TURMIX *Music Bar*
☎ 605 31 93 97; C del Dr Chiarri 8;
🕐 11.30pm-3.30am Wed-Sat; 🚌 5
A bar with resident DJ, Turmix
blasts out the best of rock every
Friday and Saturday. Wednesday is
reggae night and Thursday, strictly
techno and electronic. There's one
room for chilling out and one for
dancing, each clad in psychedelic
artwork.

>CENTRO HISTÓRICO NORTH

In the Centro Histórico, Valencia's three main squares fall like teardrops on the map: Plaza de la Virgen, overlooked by the church of the Virgen de los Desamperados (Virgin of the Dispossessed); Plaza de la Reina, dominated at its northern end by the baroque door of the cathedral, ringed by restaurants and cafes and marred by traffic; and, southwards, Plaza del Ayuntamiento.

Within its bounds are La Lonja, a reminder of Valencia's 15th-century golden age, and Mercado Central, Europe's largest fresh produce market.

Valencia's heart has throbbed here since Roman times. With most of the major historical sights, it's busy and respectable by day. By night it's a play-boy, with lots of eating options, from hole-in-the-wall fill-you-ups to elegant dining experiences. Bars run the gamut from dark and grungy to palaces for gaze-upon-me *pijos,* the rich and beautiful who come here to play.

CENTRO HISTÓRICO NORTH

◉ SEE
Almudín	1	D2
Baños del Almirante	2	E3
Cathedral	3	D3
Cripta de la Cárcel de San Vicente Mártir	4	D3
Iglesia de Santa Catalina	5	C3
La Lonja	6	C3
L'Almoina	7	D2
Mercado Central	8	C4
Miguelete Bell Tower	(see 3)	
Palacio de Benicarló	9	D1
Palacio Joan de Valeriola	10	B3
Plaza Redonda	11	C4
San Juan del Hospital	12	E3

🏃 DO
Carriage Rides	13	D3

🛍 SHOP
Bodega Baviera	(see 34)	
Bugalú	14	C3
Cactus	15	C3
Carolina Herrera	16	D4
Casa de los Dulces	17	D1
Cestería Alemany	18	D3
Guantes Camps	19	D3
Hakuna Matata	20	C3
Madame Bugalú	21	B3
Monki	22	C3
Opera Prima	23	C3
Pont des Arts	24	E3
Retal Reciclaje Creativo	25	C3
Turrones Ramos	26	C4
Zak Kolel	27	C3

🍴 EAT
Bar Pilar	28	B3
Bodeguilla del Gato	29	C3
Boing Boing	30	E3
Caminos	31	D3
Cien Montaditos	32	D3
El Molinón	33	B3
Espaivisor	34	C3
La Lola	35	D3
La Pappardella	36	D3
La Taberna de Marisa	37	B2
Messana	(see 29)	
San Nicolás	38	C3
Seu-Xerea	39	D2
Tasca Ángel	40	C3

🍸 DRINK
Café de las Horas	41	D2
Café Infanta	42	B2
Café Lisboa	43	C3
Café-Bar Negrito	44	C3
Enópata	45	D3
Horchatería de Santa Catalina	46	D4
Horchatería el Siglo	47	D3
Lounge	48	C3
Zumería Naturalia	49	D4

★ PLAY
Calcatta	50	D3
Radio City	51	B3

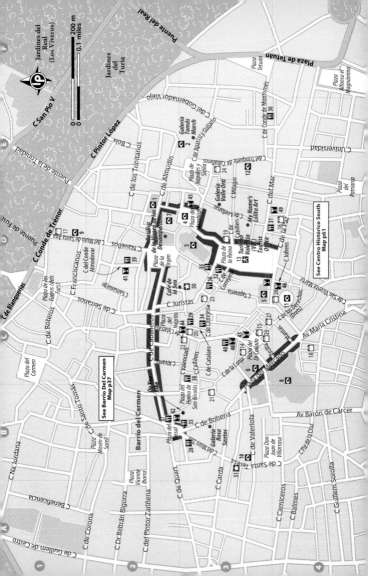

◉ SEE

◉ ALMUDÍN

☎ 96 352 54 78 ext 4521; C del Almudín; €2; ☽ 10am-2pm & 4.30-8.30pm Tue-Sat, 10am-3pm Sun; 🚌 70, 81

The 15th-century Almudín, nowadays an art gallery for large exhibitions, originally served as the city's granary, storing wheat brought in from the surrounding countryside. Writing high up on the interior walls indicates the level each year's grain reached and where it was harvested.

◉ BAÑOS DEL ALMIRANTE

☎ 605 27 57 84; C de los Baños del Almirante 3-5; admission free; ☽ 9.30am-2pm & 6-8pm Tue-Sat, 10am-2pm Sun; 🚌 70, 81

These Arab-style baths, built in 1313 shortly after the Reconquest, functioned continuously as public bathing facilities until 1959. There's an excellent audiovisual presentation with optional English commentary and guided visits every half hour.

◉ CATHEDRAL

Entrance on Plaza de la Reina; cathedral €4 incl audioguide, Miguelete bell tower €2; ☽ cathedral 10am-5.30/6.30pm Mon-Sat, 2-5.30/6.30pm Sun, Miguelete bell tower 10am-7pm Mon-Sat, 10am-1pm & 5-7pm Sun; 🚌 70, 81

Valencia's cathedral was erected on the site of the Muslim city's main mosque shortly after the city was reconquered from the Moors in 1238. Much modified over the cen-

The ornate interior of Valencia's cathedral holds exquisite art

turies, it's a microcosm of Valencia's architectural history. The Puerta del Palau is purest Romanesque. The dome, tower and Puerta de los Apóstoles – venue every Thursday at noon for the Tribunal de las Aguas (Water Court; p50) – are Gothic; the presbytery and main entrance on Plaza de la Reina are baroque; and there are a couple of Renaissance chapels inside. For more details, see p12.

◉ CRIPTA DE LA CÁRCEL DE SAN VICENTE MÁRTIR
☎ 96 394 14 17; Plaza del Arzobispo 1; €2; ◷ 10am-2pm & 5-8pm Tue-Sat, 10am-2.30pm Sun; 🚌 70, 81
Reputedly a prison for the 4th-century martyr San Vicente, the city's patron saint, the much-damaged crypt's interest lies in its excellent 25-minute multimedia show recounting Valencia's history and the saint's life and particularly gory death. Phone or call by the Museo de la Ciudad, opposite, to reserve the English version.

◉ IGLESIA DE SANTA CATALINA
Plaza de Santa Catalina; admission free; ◷ 10.30am-1.30pm & 5.30-7pm; 🚌 8, 81
This church, badly knocked about in the civil war, is starkly impressive inside. It's dwarfed by the striking late-17th-century hex-

SAN VICENTE MÁRTIR'S LEFT ARM
In a case behind the cathedral's main altar lies a withered and much-travelled relic. San Vicente was martyred around 304 and his body dismembered. In 1108, Teudovildo, the then bishop of Valencia, packed the arm in his baggage for protection as he set out on pilgrimage for Jerusalem. But before reaching the Holy Land the bishop died, in Bari on Italy's Adriatic coast. The arm spent several centuries in a convent in Venice and was finally returned to Valencia in 1970 by its most recent owner, an Italian from Padua.

agonal baroque bell tower. One of Valencia's best-known landmarks, it rivals the cathedral's Miguelete bell tower as a symbol of the city.

◉ LA LONJA
Plaza del Mercado; admission free; ◷ 10am-2pm & 4.30-8.30pm Tue-Sat, 10am-3pm Sun; 🚌 7, 81
This splendid Unesco World Heritage site was once Valencia's silk and general commodity exchange. For many, it's the city's finest building, and you'll understand why. For more information, see p18.

◉ L'ALMOINA
☎ 96 208 41 73; Plaza de L'Almoina; €2; ◷ 10am-2pm & 4.30-8.30pm Tue-Sat, 10am-3pm Sun; 🚌 70, 81
Guided visits, available in English, take you down to extensive

subterranean remains here at the very heart of Roman, Visigoth and Muslim Valencia. It's not easy to decipher the jumble of foundations, despite video displays and the guides' efforts. A pity that you have to proceed at their pace, rather than browsing freely.

◉ MERCADO CENTRAL
☎ 96 382 91 01; www.mercado centralvalencia.es, in Spanish; Plaza del Mercado; ✆ 8am-2.30pm Mon-Sat; 🚌 7, 81

What a delight of smells and sights! With nearly 900 active stalls, it claims to be Europe's largest indoor market. Size apart, it's a splendid place to browse around, sniff deeply and buy at modest prices. For details, see p15.

◉ PALACIO DE BENICARLÓ
C del Muro de Santa Ana; 🚌 5, 80

This late-Gothic 15th-century palace was once the family home of the Borjas (known in English as the infamous Borgia popes). Nowadays it's the seat of the Cortes, parliament of the Valencia region.

◉ PALACIO JOAN DE VALERIOLA
☎ 96 338 12 15; www.chirivellasoriano .org; C de Valeriola 13; ✆ 10am-2pm & 5-8pm Tue-Sat, 10am-2pm Sun; 🚌 7, 81

A 14th-century palace, sensitively restored as a contemporary art gallery that houses temporary exhibitions. Subtle lighting and the extensive use of glass complement perfectly the sweeping gothic arches of the ground floor and the slender stone windows, polychrome beams and coffered ceilings of its upper storeys.

◉ PLAZA REDONDA
🚌 8, 81

This mid-19th-century circular space was constructed on the site of the Mercado Central's

TRIBUNAL DE LAS AGUAS
For more than 1000 years, as the bell tolls the 12 strokes of noon each Thursday, this Water Court, Europe's oldest legal institution, sits in judgement outside the cathedral's Puerta de los Apóstoles. The eight members of the tribunal in their black peasant smocks each represent one of the main water channels that irrigate the *huerta*, the rich, fertile agricultural land around the city. They're here to settle local farmers' water disputes. Proceedings are in *valenciano* and exclusively oral – no written record is kept – and fines are expressed in *lliures valencianes*, a long-defunct local currency. In reality, there are rarely any complaints and it's all rather anticlimactic.

WATCH THE BIRDIE

Look up at the cockatoo (or could it be budgie?), green with verdigris, above the central market. According to legend, desperate fathers from the poverty-stricken villages of inland Aragón would bring to the big city a son they could no longer afford to feed. 'Look at that strange bird up there,' the father would say. Then, as the child gazed upwards, Dad would slip away into the crowd. And the boy, a de facto orphan, would find work as a market porter or day labourer – if luck was on his side.

former slaughterhouse. Around the perimeter stalls sell bits, bobs, buttons and bows and locally made crafts and ceramics, while lacemakers chat and throw their bobbins on Thursday from 10am to noon. It was undergoing radical renovation when we last passed.

⊙ SAN JUAN DEL HOSPITAL

☎ 96 392 29 65; C del Trinquete de Caballeros 5; ⏲ 9.30am-1.30pm & 5-9pm Mon-Sat, 11am-9pm Sun; Ⓜ Colón
Valencia's oldest church was founded in 1238, the year the city was recaptured from the Muslims. After it was vandalised in the Spanish Civil War, the church was restored to its original simple, mainly Gothic form. Highlights are the 13th-century murals in the chapel left of the altar and, at the

rear, a 12th-century Virgin and fine three-piece crucifixion.

🏃 DO
🏇 CARRIAGE RIDES

Plaza de La Reina; 🚌 80, 81
Hire a horse-drawn carriage in Plaza de la Reina and clip-clop around the Centro Histórico, lording it over the pedestrians below. A 40-minute trip costs €30 for up to five passengers. Simply turn up or reserve at the Turismo Valencia office just across the square.

🛍 SHOP
🏠 BODEGA BAVIERA *Wines*

☎ 96 391 80 60; C de Correjería 40; ⏲ 10am-3pm & 6-10pm Mon-Sat; 🚌 28, 81
Vicente Gabarda, 40 years in business, is hugely knowledgable about his stock, which he tracks from a thick, battered ringfile, scrawling his labels in felt-tip pen. This emporium for alcohol teems with pleasurable surprises such as an impressive range of malt whiskies, brandies and liqueurs and the best of Spanish vintages.

🏠 BUGALÚ *Fashion, Accessories*

☎ 96 391 84 49; C de la Lonja 6; ⏲ 10am-2pm & 5-8.30pm Mon-Sat; 🚌 60, 81
Rummage through Bugalú's rich potpourri of bags, badges, belts,

bracelets and other accessories or try on a sample of its hip, mainly casual clothing for him or her. Madame Bugalú (opposite), just along the street, stocks more sophisticated womenswear.

☐ CACTUS *Women's Clothing*
☎ 96 391 82 19; C de los Derechos 38; ⏱ 11am-2pm & 5-8.30pm Mon-Sat; 🚌 60, 81

Maureen O'Callaghan (Spanish as they come despite her Celtic name) sells her own designs and also scours Asia, Europe and her homeland for fetching women's fashions and accessories, attractively displayed against a sober wooden background.

☐ CAROLINA HERRERA
Women's Clothing, Men's Clothing
☎ 96 315 31 64; C de la Paz 5; ⏱ 10am-2pm & 4.30-8.30pm Mon-Sat; 🚌 8, 31

You'll need to flex your credit card at this upmarket outlet of modish Venezuelan designer Carolina Herrera. Downstairs it's belts, suits, jackets and slick casual shirts for him. Climb the stairs for fancy frocks and chic feminine frivolities.

☐ CASA DE LOS DULCES
Chocolate & Sweets
☎ 96 391 93 41; C del Muro de Santa Ana 6; ⏱ 9.30am-2pm & 4.30-9pm Mon-Sat, 9am-3pm & 5-9pm Sun; 🚌 5, 80

The Sweet House, known to three generations of children as Casa de los Caramelos, abounds in technicolour lollipops, sweets and candies. More than 100 glinting glass jars each hold a different variety of confectionary. This place is a paradise for children and, ultimately, dentists.

☐ CESTERÍA ALEMANY
Arts & Crafts, Gifts & Souvenirs
☎ 96 352 11 92; C de Liñan 8; ⏱ 9.30am-1.30pm & 4.30-8pm Mon-Fri, 10am-2pm Sat; 🚌 7, 81

This wonderfully cluttered shop sells everything fashioned from whippy wood and straw: baskets, boxes, trunks, screens and more. Its *alpargatas* (lightweight esparto grass slippers; €7) make original presents and will be easily tucked into your luggage. Further along the same street, **El Globo** (C del Músico Peydro 16), more cramped, piles its wicker goods just as high.

ALPARGATAS

A pair of *alpargatas*, traditional Valencian farmer's footwear – canvas on top with a sole of dried, woven grasses and bound to the ankle by cross-gartered tape – makes an original present, lightweight in your luggage, for the folks back home, and a practical alternative to sandals, especially where it's sandy or dusty.

Baskets galore at Cestería Alemany

📅 GUANTES CAMPS *Fashion*
☎ 96 392 39 81; Plaza de la Reina 18;
🕑 9am-1.30pm & 4.30-8pm Mon-Sat;
🚌 28, 81

This shop specialises in gloves for all occasions. The salesperson will rest your elbow on a cushion and ease a glove on for size. Call by in summer too and inspect the impressive range of fans. There's a similar shop (same name, different owners) at C de San Vicente Mártir 3.

📅 HAKUNA MATATA
Jewellery, Gifts & Souvenirs
☎ 96 391 45 37; C de Calatrava 4;
🕑 11.30am-2.30pm & 5-8.30pm Mon-Sat; 🚌 28, 81

For original gifts, pass by Hakuna Matata and watch Mauricio, its owner, at work as he fashions his own jewellery (he can create a piece to your design in three days, or mail it on to you). He also buys in jewellery and other artefacts directly from fellow artists.

📅 MADAME BUGALÚ
Women's Clothing
☎ 96 315 44 76; C de Danzas 3;
🕑 10am-2pm & 5-8.30pm Mon-Sat;
🚌 5B, 81

No more than 100m from its mother shop, Bugalú (p51), Madame Bugalú is an altogether sassier, more sophisticated boutique for womenswear.

☐ MONKI *Women's Clothing*
☎ 96 392 45 16; C de Calatrava 11;
🕑 11am-2pm & 5-9pm Mon-Sat,
11.30am-3pm Sun; 🚍 5B, 81

Lisa, the canny Irish owner, has
a keen eye for fads and fashions,
buying in from local designers
and combing Europe for striking
womenswear. Check out too Mini-
monki, her new line for kids.

☐ OPERA PRIMA *Delicatessen*
☎ 96 391 98 68; C de Correjería 9;
🕑 11am-2pm & 5-8.30pm Mon-Sat;
🚍 5B, 81

This chic, brightly lit delicatessen
where classical music plays (Opera
Prima because it's the two young
owners' first business venture)
offers top quality, attractively
packaged products – ideal as gifts.

☐ PONT DES ARTS
Jewellery, Gifts & Souvenirs
☎ 96 392 56 13; www.lepontdesarts.es,
in Spanish; Plaza de Nápoles y Sicilia 1;
🕑 10am-2pm & 5-8pm Mon-Fri, 5-8pm
Sat, 11am-2pm Sun; Ⓜ Colón

This elegant boutique with its
attractively crafted contemporary
French jewellery and exclusive
silver pieces from Nepal is
perfect as a present for someone
special. Browsing over, relax in
its intimate tea house that offers
nearly 50 varieties of tea for sale
or sipping.

TURRÓN

This particularly lipsmacking variant
upon nougat makes a great locally
made, handy-sized present. Traditionally eaten around Christmas time, it's a
treat at any time of the year. There are
two main kinds: *Turrón de Jijona*, soft
and fudgelike, and *Turrón de Alicante*,
altogether crisper and crunchier. **Tur-
rones Ramos** (☎ 96 392 33 98; C de
Sombería 11; 🕑 10am-noon & 5-8pm
Mon-Fri) sells *turrón* that comes from its
own factory in Jijona.

☐ RETAL RECICLAJE CREATIVO
Men's Clothing, Women's Clothing
☎ 96 391 28 20; www.retalreciclaje
creativo.com; C de los Derechos 25;
🕑 11am-2pm & 5-8.30pm Mon-Sat;
🚍 5B, 81

Retal Creative Recycling is the
initiative of Paolo Coppolella and
Paola Pucci, a pair of exciting
young Italian designers. Here in
their studio and retail outlet, they
fashion one-off, reasonably priced
garments for both sexes, using
offcuts and end-of-line fabrics
(hence the 'Recycling' of their
name).

☐ ZAK KOLEL
Women's Clothing, Jewellery
☎ 96 392 21 59; C de los Derechos 32;
🕑 11am-2pm & 5.30-9pm Mon-Sat;
🚍 5B, 81

Named after the Mayan goddess of love, Zak Kolel is both a retail outlet for the creations of Hakuna Matata (p53) and a boutique with a smart line in clothes and accessories.

🍴 EAT

🍴 BAR PILAR *Tapas* €
☎ 96 391 04 97; C del Moro Zeit 13; ⏰ noon–midnight; 🚌 7, 81

Cramped, earthy Bar Pilar is a great place to come to for hearty tapas and *clóchinas,* small, juicy local mussels, available between June and August. For the rest of the year, they serve *mejillones,* altogether fatter if less tasty. Ask for an *entero,* a platterful in a spicy broth that you scoop up with a spare shell. At the bar, etiquette demands that you dump your empty shells in the plastic trough at your feet.

🍴 BODEGUILLA DEL GATO
Tapas €€
☎ 96 391 82 35; C de Catalans 10; ⏰ 8.30pm–midnight; 🚌 5B, 7

Never mind the tacky bullfight poster and heterogeneous decorations. This thoroughly Valencian, bare-brick place serves excellent salads and tapas (try, for example, the wild boar chorizo) and keeps a carefully chosen wine list.

🍴 BOING BOING
Mediterranean Fusion €€
☎ 96 392 02 02; C del Conde de Montornés 8; ⏰ lunch & dinner Mon–Fri, dinner Sat; 🚌 8, 70

Pause for an aperitif at the softly lit red and black bar of this hip venue, then mount the stairs to the all-white restaurant with its exposed ducting and mellow brickwork. Boing Boing is ideal for couples since all dishes are designed to be shared. To order, simply tick/check items on your menu sheet.

🍴 CAMINOS
Mediterranean €€
☎ 96 315 47 58; cnr C del Mar & Luis Vives; menu €18; ⏰ 8am–5pm Mon–Fri plus 8pm–midnight Fri & Sat; 🚌 5, 80

You don't immediately think of a trade union serving gourmet food. But this quality restaurant and cafe – belonging to the Association of Road, Canal & Port Engineers, with its bright, airy, contemporary decor – is a great option. Open to all, it has an ample à la carte choice and also serves an excellent value lunch *menú* (€18).

🍴 CIEN MONTADITOS
Tapas €
☎ 96 391 92 27; Plaza de la Reina 10; ⏰ 11.30am–midnight 🚌 8, 70

You've a choice of precisely 100 fillings (€1.20 to €1.50) for your *montadito* (miniroll). Fill in the order form at your table, choose a drink, present it at the counter and listen for your name to be called. Speedy and superb value, though it doesn't accept reservations.

🍴 EL MOLINÓN *Tapas* €
☎ 96 391 15 38; C de Bolsería 40; 🕑 lunch & dinner; 🚌 5B, 81

El Molinón, all stone and slate with simple wooden furniture, serves more than 50 kinds of tapas. The wine list chalked up on the wall is fine, but you really ought to invest in a bottle of scrumpy cider from Asturias, in Spain's northwest. Poured from a height, it's a spectacle as well as a drink.

🍴 ESPAIVISOR *Vegetarian* €€
☎ 96 392 23 99; www.espaivisor.com, in Spanish; C de Correjería 40; 🕑 dinner Tue-Sat; 🚌 28, 81; 🅥 ☐

In a city with few vegetarian options, this tiny restaurant and photographic gallery stands out. Dishes are enticingly photographed (no surprise that owner Pep Benlloch is a professional) and the innovative menu is in Spanish and English. Free wi-fi too.

🍴 LA LOLA
Mediterranean Fusion €€
☎ 96 391 80 45; www.lalolarestaurante .com, in Spanish; Subida del Toledano 8; 🕑 lunch & dinner Mon-Sat; 🚌 5B, 81

El Molinón for tapas

Up an alley beside the cathedral, here's a very suave number, where cool jazz trills and the white bar, walls and furnishings contrast with stark reds, blacks and giant polka dots. Desserts in particular (such as orange crème brûlée with *turrón* ice cream) are wickedly tempting. There's also regular live jazz and flamenco.

🍴 LA PAPPARDELLA
Italian   €€
☎ 96 391 89 15; C de Bordadores 5; ⏱ lunch & dinner; 🚌 5B, 81

La Pappardella, with its ultrafriendly, speedy staff, offers authentic Italian cuisine, reasonably priced. Built on two floors around a central patio, it's agreeably broken up into smaller areas and has a small street terrace.

🍴 LA TABERNA DE MARISA
Tapas   €
☎ 96 392 18 27; C de Caballeros 47; ⏱ 1-4pm & 9pm-midnight Mon-Fri, 8pm-midnight Sat; 🚌 5B, 81

Dine intimately upstairs or pick tapas at the busy bar, where fat hams hang beside giant crusty loaves of bread. Ingredients and wines (see the selection of the week on the giant chalkboard) are prime quality, the *morcilla de Burgos* (roundels of black pudding) is sublime and jolly Marisa will give you a warm welcome.

🍴 MESSANA
International   €€
☎ 96 315 59 75; www.restaurant emessana.com, in Spanish; C de Catalans 8; ⏱ lunch & dinner Tue-Sat; 🚌 5B, 81

This appealing restaurant is all bare brick, exposed beams and wall-to-ceiling artwork. Savour, for example, the tenderest of thick beef steak followed by a delightfully creative dessert. There's an excellent selection of accompanying wines, about which staff are knowledgable.

🍴 SAN NICOLÁS
Fish   €€
☎ 96 391 59 84; Plaza del Horno de San Nicolás 8; ⏱ lunch & dinner Tue-Sat & lunch Sun; 🚌 5B, 81

You're guaranteed the freshest of fish, bought from San Nicolás' own suppliers in the smaller fishing ports up and down the coast. Don't be baffled by their names, some obscure even to locals. Your friendly hosts will produce an illustrated guide with multilingual terms.

🍴 SEU-XEREA
Mediterranean Fusion   €€
☎ 96 392 40 00; www.seuxerea.com; C del Conde Almodóvar 4; ⏱ lunch & dinner Mon-Fri, dinner Sat; 🚌 5, 95

Welcoming Seu-Xerea is favourably quoted in almost every English-language press article about Valencia. The creative, regularly changing à la carte menu features dishes both international and rooted in

Spain. It does a warmly recommended *menú del día* (lunch €22, dinner €30). Wines, selected by the chef-owner, a qualified sommelier, are uniformly excellent.

🍴 TASCA ÁNGEL *Tapas* €
☎ 96 391 78 35; C de la Purísima 2; ◷ 10.30am-3pm & 7.30-11.30pm Mon-Sat; 🚌 60, 81

If the sound and scent of fresh, boned sardines sizzling on the griddle drives you wild, call by Tasca Ángel, more than 60 years in business, scarcely more than a hole in the wall and something of a Valencian institution. Wash it down with a glass of chilled white wine.

🍸 DRINK

🍸 CAFÉ DE LAS HORAS
Cafe, Cocktail Bar
☎ 96 391 73 36; C del Conde de Almodóvar 1; ◷ 4pm-1.30am Sun-Thu, 4pm-3am Fri & Sat; 🚌 5, 95

This high-baroque setting demands a special drink. An exotic cocktail? Or something from the long list of brandies and sparkling wines? If the incense brings on the sneezes, opt for the streetside terrace. On Mondays at 8pm there's international conversation in English.

🍸 CAFÉ INFANTA *Bar, Cafe*
☎ 96 392 16 23; Plaza del Tossal 3; ◷ 4pm-2am; 🚌 5B, 81

Café Infanta is one of a cluster of enticing choices around Plaza del Tossal. Good for a terrace drink (look first; this side of the otherwise respectable square is favoured by dossers and drunks), its interior has cinema memorabilia, display cases, publicity photos and posters.

🍸 CAFÉ LISBOA *Bar, Cafe*
☎ 96 391 94 84; Plaza del Doctor Collado 9; ◷ 9am-1am Sun-Thu, 9am-2.30am Fri & Sat; 🚌 7, 81

The innards of this lively, student-oriented bar are a bit cramped and constricting; its large, street-side terrace is the place to sip your drink. The bulletin board is a palimpsest of small ads for apartment shares and language tuition.

🍸 CAFÉ-BAR NEGRITO
Bar, Cafe
☎ 96 391 42 33; Plaza del Negrito; ◷ 3pm-3.30am; 🚌 5B, 81

In summer, every square metre of small, busy Plaza del Negrito, ringed by bars, is a tangle of chairs and tables. Café-Bar Negrito, recently redesigned and a local favourite, traditionally attracts an intellectual, left-wing crowd. You'll be lucky to find a seat after 9pm.

🍸 ENÓPATA *Wine Bar*
☎ 96 325 91 50; www.enopata.com, in Spanish; Plaza del Arzobispo 5; ◷ lunch Mon-Sat, dinner Thu-Sat; 🚌 5, 95

HORCHATA

This sweet, opaque, very Valencian drink is made from pressed *chufas* (tiger nuts), into which you dip large finger-shaped buns called *fartons*; both name and taste are to savour. To sample this drink in the heart of town, two traditional places, facing each other and both tiled from floor to ceiling, are **Horchatería de Santa Catalina** (Map p61, C1; ☎ 96 391 23 79; Plaza de Santa Catalina 6; ☼ 8am-9pm) and **Horchatería el Siglo** (☎ 96 391 84 66; Plaza de Santa Catalina 11; ☼ 8am-9pm Sun-Fri).

The message curling around the walls of this very superior wine bar, run by committed oenophile, Juan Ferrer, reads 'Life's too short to waste by drinking bad wines'. The setting is welcoming and there's a great range of mains (around €15).

☯ THE LOUNGE *Bar, Cafe*
☎ 96 391 80 94; www.theloungecafe bar.com; C de Estameñaría Vieja 2; ☼ 5pm-1.30am; 🚌 7, 81; ☐
Run by Fiona from Ireland, this particularly friendly bar is a popular haunt of foreign students. There's free wi-fi, an internet terminal and, on Mondays, a Spanish-English language interchange. It also does tempting snacks and shakes some mean cocktails.

☯ ZUMERÍA NATURALIA *Bar*
☎ 96 391 12 11; C del Mar 12; ☼ 5pm-1am Mon-Sat, 5-10.15pm Sun; 🚌 27, 81
Measures of juicy, fruity cocktails, with or without an alcoholic kick, are huge, in glasses the size of goldfish bowls. It's popular with couples, gazing deep into each other's eyes. Wriggling into a comfortable posture in the deep wicker chairs is an art in itself.

⭐ PLAY

⭐ CALCATTA *Club*
C del Reloj Viejo 4; minimum €8; ☼ 2-7am Fri & Sat; 🚌 28, 81
For drinks, get your card punched at this long-established club, housed in a 15th-century building. Its three floors overlook the interior patio and dance floor. The music is a mix of everything from all eras. The DJ is normally open to requests.

⭐ RADIO CITY *Club*
☎ 96 391 41 51; www.radiocityvalencia .com, in Spanish; C de Santa Teresa 19; ☼ 10pm-3.30am; 🚌 7, 81
Almost as much mini–cultural centre as club, Radio City, always seething, knows how to pull in the punters with activities including flamenco (11pm Tuesdays), seasonal theatre, cinema and dancing to an eclectic mix. Pick up a flyer here for its younger sister, Music Box (p45).

>CENTRO HISTÓRICO SOUTH

North and South of the historic centre are simply our division of convenience to make navigation in the guide and on the ground easier. In fact, you'll slip imperceptibly between one and the other, finding each equally rich in restaurants and contemporary art galleries.

There's something special about shopping in this southern part, though: C de Colón, the city's busiest shopping street, is lined with major Spanish chains and elegant clothes shops for him and her. By contrast, shorter C del Poeta Querol is the place for exclusive, top-of-the-range brands. More intimately, small, local single-product shops selling gloves, shawls, hats or chocolate still manage to survive the stiff commercial competition.

Architecturally, the 19th-century facade of the main post office vies in splendour with that of the city's Town Hall, opposite. They seem to stare at each other in ongoing rivalry across the busy Plaza del Ayuntamiento.

CENTRO HISTÓRICO SOUTH

⚙ SEE
Galería La Nave	1	E2
Galería Luis Adelantado	2	E2
Main Post Office	3	D3
Museo del Patriarca	4	E2
Museo Histórico Municipal	............(see 8)	
Museo Nacional de Cerámica	..................(see 5)	
Palacio del Marqués de Dos Aguas	5	D2
Plaza del Ayuntamiento	6	C2
Plaza Redonda	7	C1
Town Hall	8	C3

🛍 SHOP
Alex Vidal	9	D2
Añadas de España	10	C3
Armand Basi	11	E3
Beguer	12	E3
Camper	13	E3
Camper	14	D1
Casa de los Falleros	15	B3
Cuchillería Eureka	16	D1
Guantes Camps	..........(see 16)
Librería Patagonia	17	B2
Lladró	18	D2
Malasaña	19	C2
Mango	20	E3
Mango	21	E2
Massimo Dutti	22	D3
Massimo Dutti	23	D4
Navarro	24	C3
Nela	25	D1
Purificación García	26	D1
Purificación García	27	E3
Rosalén	28	C2
Santa María Novella	29	D1
Sombreros Albero	30	D4
Valencia Club de Fútbol Shop	31	E2
Xocoa	32	D1
Zara	33	D3
Zara Home	34	E4

🍴 EAT
Commo	35	D3
FresCo	36	C2
Ginger Loft Café	37	D1
La Utielana	38	D2
Neco	39	D3
Palacio de la Bellota	40	D3
Sagardí	41	C1

🍸 DRINK
Cafe de la Nau	42	E2
Café Rialto	...............(see 46)
Octubre	43	C1

⭐ PLAY
Filmoteca	..................(see 46)
La Claca	....................(see 16)
Teatro Olympia	44	C2
Teatro Principal	45	D2
Teatro Rialto	46	D2

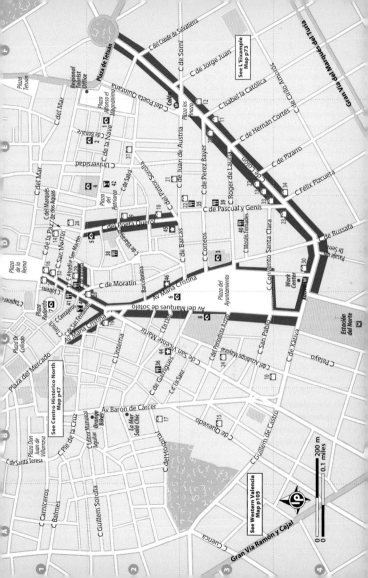

SEE

MAIN POST OFFICE

Plaza del Ayuntamiento 24; 🕐 **8.30am-8.30pm Mon-Fri, 9.30am-2pm Sat;** Ⓜ **Xàtiva**

Drop into Correos, Valencia's neo-classical main post office, to admire its spaciousness and superb stained-glass ceiling. The winged angels and sculpted train on its roof could perhaps get letters more swiftly to their destination than today's service. Let children pop postcards into the mouths of the two resplendent lion letter boxes on C de Correos.

MUSEO DEL PATRIARCA

☎ **96 351 41 76; C de la Nave 1; €2;** 🕐 **11am-1.30pm;** Ⓜ **Colón**

This bijou ecclesiastical museum is particularly strong on Spanish and Flemish Renaissance painting, with several canvases each by Juan de Juanes and Ribalta and a trio of El Grecos. The desiccated alligator above the church door is an exhortation to silence; the alligator, unlike the church's more garrulous parishioners, has no tongue.

PALACIO DEL MARQUÉS DE DOS AGUAS & MUSEO NACIONAL DE CERÁMICA

☎ **96 351 63 92; C del Poeta Querol 2; €2 (free Sat pm & Sun);** 🕐 **10am-2pm & 4-8pm Tue-Sat, 10am-2pm Sun;** 🚌 **8, 81**

A pair of muscled alabaster caryatids prop up the doorway of this extravagantly rococo palace. Within, the National Ceramics Museum charts the history of china and pottery from Roman times to the present day, including ample representation from the local centres of Manises and Paterna, major ceramics producers to this day.

PLAZA DEL AYUNTAMIENTO

Ⓜ **Xàtiva**

If Plaza de la Virgen is the heart of Valencia's spiritual life, here, where Town Hall and post office face each other in permanent stand-off, is its temporal equivalent. Fountains dance and spurt and precisely 13 flower shops display their floral best.

TOWN HALL

Plaza del Ayuntamiento 1; free; 🕐 **9am-2pm;** Ⓜ **Xàtiva**

Valencia's handsome neoclassical Ayuntamiento dominates the square that takes its name. Within is the **Museo Histórico Municipal** (admission free; 🕐 9am-2pm Mon-Fri), a repository of items important to the city's identity, such as the sword that Jaime I is reputed to have brandished when defeating the Muslim occupiers, and a fascinating 1704 map of Valencia, drafted by Padre Tosca. Enter via the door just south of the main steps.

Nacho Valle
Owner, Galería Valle Ortí (p69), Turmix music bar (p45) and a Japanese restaurant. He's also an active DJ around town.

Tell me about Galería Valle Ortí. Well, I began working with my father, who established the gallery back in the 1970s. After he died in 2001, I gave it a new ultracontemporary focus, promoting emerging young artists. **And Turmix?** That came later, in 2004, letting me indulge in my other passion – rock and roll. **Where do you go for a good night out?** The Valencia scene is relatively small and we DJs and club owners all know and visit each other. Of the discotecas, my favourites are Murray Club (p103) and The Mill Clubs (p95). **And eating out?** I enjoy cooking, but when I do eat out with friends, I go to Tasca Ángel (p58) or Casa Guillermo (p92) for tapas. For a full meal, we'll visit Seu-Xerea (p57) or Dukala (p109) for its great Moroccan cuisine or maybe Espaivisor (p56), an excellent vegetarian option.

🛍 SHOP

🛍 ALEX VIDAL *Fashion*
☎ 96 351 32 83; www.alexvidal.es; C de Salvá 2; ⏰ 10.15am-1.15pm & 5-8pm Mon-Fri, 10.30am-2pm Sat; Ⓜ Colón
Branch of local designer Alex Vidal (p74).

🛍 AÑADAS DE ESPAÑA
Delicatessen
☎ 96 353 38 45; www.lasanadas.es, in Spanish; C de Xàtiva 3; ⏰ 9am-9pm Mon-Sat; Ⓜ Xàtiva
The Seasons of Spain is a true temple to gourmet food. It carries the very best in cheeses, cold meats, patés and sausages and does delicious cakes and desserts. There's also an ample wine selection.

🛍 ARMAND BASI
Men's Clothing, Women's Clothing
☎ 96 351 48 06; C de Colón 52; ⏰ 10am-8.30pm Mon-Sat; Ⓜ Colón
Here on the main shopping street is the only Valencia branch (its power base is in Catalonia) of this hip Spanish chain specialising in trim casualwear for men and women.

🛍 BEGUER *Shoes, Accessories*
☎ 96 394 25 47; C de Colón 58; ⏰ 10am-8.45pm Mon-Sat; Ⓜ Xàtiva
Beguer is a local enterprise that manufactures in Torrente, a dormi-

> **INSIDER TRADING: ALEX VIDAL STOCKS**
> Psst, here's a tip. Find the first building on the left (No 1) of Pasaje Dr Serra, a covered gallery running alongside the bullring. Go up the stairs to the 1st floor and there, in an unassuming office (No 3), you'll find **Alex Vidal Stocks** (☎ 96 352 87 55; ⏰ 10am-1.30pm & 4.30-8.30pm Mon-Fri, 10am-2pm Sat), discreet outlet of the renowned Valencian designer (p74), where discounts on previous year's stock *begin* at 60%.

tory town southwest of Valencia. Its main line is fashionable shoes and boots for men and women, supplemented by a range of classy bags. There's also a branch at C de Hernán Cortés 16.

🛍 CAMPER *Shoes*
☎ 96 353 39 55; www.camper.com; C de Colón 13; ⏰ 10am-9pm Mon-Sat; Ⓜ Xàtiva
Camper, the shoe company that is based in Mallorca, is something of a Spanish institution. But just because it's popular doesn't mean that its output is run-of-the-mill. Choose what fits you and you'll dance out, toes tapping with satisfaction. It has another shop at the corner of C de la Paz and C del Marqués de dos Aguas.

🏠 CASA DE LOS FALLEROS
Women's Clothing

☎ 96 352 14 00; C de Quevedo 6;
🕐 9.30am-1.30pm & 4.30-8pm Mon-Fri,
10am-2pm & 4.30-8pm Sat; Ⓜ Xàtiva,
Ángel Guimerà

Here's the place to buy a traditional *fallera* (female festival participant) dress and accessories, or simply see roll upon roll of embroidered, sequined cloth and racks of off-the peg dresses. Check your creditworthiness; a ready-made ensemble will set you back at least €800 while a special creation could climb to more than €5500.

🏠 CUCHILLERÍA EUREKA
Accessories

☎ 96 352 06 04; www.brochasdeafeitar
.com, in Spanish; C de San Vicente Mártir
3; 🕐 10am-2pm & 5-8pm Mon-Sat;
🚌 8, 81

Eureka indeed! It carries around 400 varieties of shaving brush, more toe-clippers than you have toes, plus nose tweezers and other essential accoutrements for the person about town. The window display might be a surgeon's outfitters.

🏠 LIBRERÍA PATAGONIA
Travel Bookshop

☎ 96 393 60 52; www.libreriapatagonia
.com, in Spanish; C del Hospital 1;
🕐 10am-2pm & 4.30-8.30pm Mon-Sat;
🚌 9, 81

Patagonia is an excellent travel bookshop with an unrivalled selection of maps, guidebooks, climbing and trekking manuals, mostly in Spanish. Exceptionally friendly and helpful and with a travel agency attached, it also carries guides in English, including lots of Lonely Planet titles.

🏠 LLADRÓ *Arts & Crafts*

☎ 96 351 16 25; C del Poeta Querol
9; 🕐 10am-2pm & 4-8pm Mon-Sat;
Ⓜ Colón

The sole outlet in Valencia of local ceramics giant Lladró is deliberately cited on the city's smartest street. In what is almost a mini-museum, you can browse among and purchase its winsome figurines.

LLADRÓ

More than half a century ago, the three Lladró brothers produced the first of their famed porcelain sculptures. Nowadays, their factory in Tabernes Blanques, on the northern outskirts of Valencia, employs a staff of hundreds and exports its figurines worldwide.

Free 1½-hour tours take place from 9.30am to 5pm, Monday to Friday, and until 1.30pm on Saturday. You can reserve online (www.lladro.com) or by phoning ☎ 900 21 10 10. Take the Metro to Palmaret or bus No 16. For bargains, drop into the seconds shop, nearby.

⬤ MALASAÑA *Fashion*
☎ 680 44 71 44; www.nosolocamisetas
.com, in Spanish; Plaza de Porxets 7;
🕑 10am-1.30pm & 5-8.30pm Mon-Sat;
🚌 6, 71

Tucked into tiny Plaza de Porxets, just off C de San Vicente Mártir, Malasaña sells nothing but hip T-shirts ('Besame Street', 'Web Side Story' and much more), designed and printed by a team of young Valencian artists.

⬤ MANGO
Men's Clothing, Women's Clothing
☎ 96 352 88 58; www.mango.es; C de Colón 31; 🕑 10am-9pm Mon-Sat;
Ⓜ Colón

Mango, like Zara, is a Spanish company with branches worldwide. It's a bit funkier than its rival, mixing couture with quality fabrics and department-store prices. Its other branch in central Valencia, at C de Juan de Austria 7, is just for women.

⬤ MASSIMO DUTTI
Men's Clothing, Women's Clothing
☎ 96 352 42 63; www.massimodutti
.com; C de Colón 9; 🕑 10am-9.30pm Mon-Sat; Ⓜ Xátiva

Massimo Dutti, despite the Italian name, is as Spanish as flamenco (it's part of the Zara conglomerate). There are twin shops: look left for women's clothing and right for menswear. It has another branch at C de Juan de Austria 4.

⬤ NAVARRO *Delicatessen*
☎ 96 352 28 51; C del Arzobispo Mayoral 20 & C de San Vicente Mártir 63; 🕑 9am-8.15pm Mon-Sat; Ⓜ Xátiva

Navarro, just behind the Town Hall, is Valencia's best option for vegetarian food, including organic vegetables. Within this vast ecofriendly emporium, stretching between two streets, you'll find a huge range of products from all over Europe.

⬤ PURIFICACIÓN GARCÍA
Fashion
☎ 96 352 36 06; www.purificacion
garcia.es, in Spanish; C de Colón 17, 🕑 10am-8.30pm Mon-Sat; Ⓜ Colón

A nationwide chain, yes, but one that's a great resource for smart designerwear for him and her, whether formal, informal, casual, sporty or just plain fun. There's another branch at C del Marqués de Dos Aguas 7.

⬤ SANTA MARIA NOVELLA
Perfumes
☎ 96 394 23 34; C de la Abadía de San Martín; 🕑 10am-9.30pm Mon-Sat;
🚌 6, 71

The shelves of the Valencia branch of Florence's world famous perfume shop brim with subtle scents, salts, creams, lotions, unguents, balms, honeys and jams.

☐ SOMBREROS ALBERO
Gifts & Souvenirs
☎ 96 351 22 45; C de Xàtiva 21;
🕐 10am-1.30pm & 5-8pm Mon-Sat;
Ⓜ Xàtiva

Sombreros Albero can set you up with a dapper panama, trilby, beret or bonnet. Most are knocked up locally by this small concern, run by the Albero family since 1820. There's a branch at Plaza del Mercado 9, beside the central market.

☐ VALENCIA CLUB DE FÚTBOL SHOP *Gifts & Souvenirs*
☎ 96 351 47 42; www.valenciacf.com;
C del Pintor Sorolla 25; 🕐 10am-9pm Mon-Sat; Ⓜ Colón

Anyone who is seriously soccer-crazy might want to pick up a scarf, flag, woolly hat, poster or shirt from this official club shop. You can also purchase tickets to forthcoming matches from this outlet.

Stylish headwear at the historic Sombreros Albero

NEIGHBOURHOODS

CENTRO HISTÓRICO SOUTH

🍫 XOCOA *Chocolate & Sweets*
☎ 96 351 77 39; C de San Vicente Mártir 7; ⏱ 10am-9pm; 🚌 6, 71

Drop into this sweet smelling, very central shop for the finest in quality chocolates, in blocks and boxes and fashioned into chocolate buttons, keys, CDs and contorted Kama Sutra figures.

🛍 ZARA
Men's Clothing, Women's Clothing
☎ 96 352 76 03; www.zara.com; C de Colón 11; ⏱ 10am-9pm Mon-Sat; Ⓜ Xàtiva

Zara, with several branches around town, sells smart, quality, inexpensive casuals. This main branch has both men's and women's departments and also does great gear for fashion-conscious kids.

COOL FANS, WARM SHAWLS

Two central places to pick up a special fan are **Nela** (☎ 96 392 30 23; C de San Vicente Mártir 2; ⏱ 9.45am-1.30pm & 4.15-8pm Mon-Fri, 10am-1.30pm Sat), which also does a nice line in umbrellas and walking sticks, and **Rosalén** (⏱ 96 351 14 14; ⏱ 9.45am-1.30pm & 4.15-8pm Mon-Fri, 10am-1.30pm Sat) at No 19. Both stock gorgeous Manila shawls, which vary in price from around €40 for a simple, machine-embroidered version to as much as €300 for a special silk number.

🏠 ZARA HOME *Homewares*
☎ 96 352 68 13; www.zarahome.com; C de Colón 18; ⏱ 10am-9pm Mon-Sat; Ⓜ Xàtiva

The household goods in Zara Home have the same design flair and reasonable prices as the original Zara fashion chain. If it's packed, walk to the nearby branch in L'Eixample (p78), which is equally well stocked.

🍴 EAT

🍴 COMMO *Mediterranean* €€
☎ 96 352 36 49; C de Pascual y Genís 3; ⏱ lunch Mon, lunch & dinner Tue-Sat; Ⓜ Xàtiva

The decor at this classy restaurant is minimalist. The menu changes regularly and radically to match the seasons and everything is confected on the premises from the freshest of ingredients. Not least of Commo's charms are its toilets with their wraparound mirrors.

🍴 FRESC CO *Self-Service* €
☎ 96 351 58 64; C de Garrigues 6; ⏱ 12.30-5pm & 8-11pm; Ⓜ Xàtiva; Ⓥ

Branch of the popular self-service restaurant (p80).

🍴 GINGER LOFT CAFÉ
International, Fusion €
☎ 96 352 32 43; www.thegingerloft .com; C de Vitoria 4; ⏱ 2pm-1am Mon-Sat, 12.30pm-12.30am Sun; 🚌 4, 70

CONTEMPORARY ART GALLERIES IN THE OLD TOWN

Scattered around Valencia's historic heart are most of the city's major private contemporary art galleries, all easily visited during a morning's walking.

Espaivisor (Map p47, C3; ☎ 96 392 23 99; www.espaivisor.com, in Spanish; C de Correjería 40; ☷ 5pm-midnight Tue-Fri, noon-midnight Sat; 🚍 28, 81) The display area, up on the 1st floor, may be tiny but the quality is always first class at Valencia's premier photographic gallery. Combine viewing with a tasty vegetarian dinner (see p56).

Galería La Nave (☎ 96 351 19 33; www.galerialanave.com; C de la Nave 25; ☷ 11am-2pm & 5-9pm Mon-Sat; Ⓜ Colón) Beyond her gallery's splendid stainless-steel facade are the fruits of owner María Jiménez's skill in identifying new trends.

Galería Luis Adelantado (☎ 96 351 01 79; www.luisadelantadovalencia.com; C de Bonaire 6; ☷ 10am-2pm & 4.30-8.30pm Mon-Sat; Ⓜ Colón) Luis Adelantado has displayed for more than 25 years in Valencia (and latterly in Miami too) and runs a prestigious annual competition for artists under 35.

Galería Rosa Santos (Map p47, B3; ☎ 96 392 64 17; www.rosasantos.net; C de Bolsería 21; ☷ 5-9pm Mon-Sat; 🚍 5B, 81) Rosa Santos specialises in conceptual art, usually showcasing for the first time a young, rising artist.

Galería Tomás March (Map p47, E3; ☎ 96 392 20 95; www.tomasmarch.com; C de Aparisi y Guijarro 7; ☷ 11am-2pm & 5.30-9pm Tue-Fri, noon-2pm & 6-9pm Sat; Ⓜ Colón) Tomás March runs a stable of emerging, mainly Spanish artists.

Galería Valle Ortí (Map p47, D3; ☎ 96 392 33 77; www.valleorti.com; C de Avellanas 22; ☷ 11am-2pm & 5.30-9pm Tue-Fri, 5.30-9pm Sat; 🚍 28, 81) Nacho Valle, who studied photography at Westminster University, UK, has taken over the running of this exciting, long-established gallery from the founder, his father.

My Name's Lolita Art (Map p47, D3; ☎ 96 391 13 72; www.mynameslolita.com; C de Avellanas 7; ☷ 10.30am-1.30pm & 5-8.30pm Mon-Sat; 🚍 28, 81) A gallery that promotes young artists, who then stay with the stable over the years.

Mike from Scotland and his Peruvian-Japanese partner, Santiago, run this delightful small cafe with its upstairs chill-out zone. Wines are all from the Valencia region and there's a pageful of sexy cocktails. Snack from the great selection of Spanish hams and cheeses or choose a dish from the international range of mains.

🍴 **LA UTIELANA** Spanish €
☎ 96 352 94 14; 14 Plaza de Picadero dos Aguas; ☷ lunch & dinner Mon-Fri, lunch Sat; 🚍 4, 6
Hidden away off C de Prócida, La Utielana well merits a few minutes' sleuthing. Clad in blue and white tiling and very Valencian, it offers exceptional value for money. It doesn't take reservations – if you

have to wait, grab a numbered ticket from the dispenser.

🍴 NECO *Self-Service* €
☎ 96 369 55 21; C de Pascual y Genís 9; ☽ lunch & dinner; Ⓜ Xàtiva

Neco makes a great central self-service choice. The buffet (Monday to Friday €10, Saturday and Sunday €13) is rich in salads and has plenty of options for vegetarians.

🍴 PALACIO DE LA BELLOTA
Fish, Seafood €€€
☎ 96 351 53 61; www.palaciodela bellota.es; C de Mosén Femades 7; ☽ lunch & dinner Mon-Sat; Ⓜ Xàtiva

Palacio de la Bellota is one of a cluster of superb upmarket seafood restaurants flanking this pedestrianised street. Shellfish are hauled fresh from the Mediterranean and the fish selection is also excellent. Ham as well, legs of it dangling in profusion from the ceiling. Eat inside or on the street terrace.

🍴 SAGARDÍ *Tapas* €
☎ 96 391 06 68; C de San Vicente Mártir 6; ☽ 10am-2.30am; 🚌 4, 70

Enjoy delightful tapas (from €1.20 each) downstairs. Keep the sticks that impale them since that's how the staff tots up your bill. Try the white Basque Txakoli wine or a glass of Sidra de Astigarraga, cider from the Basque country. Upstairs is the even more impressive restaurant.

Dine under maturing legs of ham at Palacio de la Bellota

CINEMA & THEATRE

In the heart of Valencia are its three main theatres for drama and an excellent art-house cinema.

Filmoteca (☎ 96 399 55 77; www.ivac-lafilmoteca.es, in Spanish; Plaza del Ayuntamiento) Screens undubbed classic, art-house and experimental films.

Teatro Olympia (☎ 96 351 73 15; C de San Vicente Mártir) Privately owned, offers an intermittent diet of comedy, safe potboilers and dance.

Teatro Principal (☎ 96 353 92 00; C de Barcas 15) Valencia's main public-sector venue for opera, theatre and dance.

Teatro Rialto (☎ 96 353 93 00) Like the Filmoteca, with which it shares premises, it belongs to the regional government. Promotes mainly local drama and dance, often in *valenciano*.

▼ DRINK

▼ CAFE DE LA NAU *Cafe*

☎ 96 386 41 79; C de La Nave 2; ⏰ 8am-8pm Mon-Fri, 8am-2pm Sat; Ⓜ Colón

Within a historic building, until recently Valencia University's rectorate and still a venue for temporary exhibitions, this cafe's tranquil, columned internal patio is ideal for unwinding after an intensive bout of shopping on nearby C de Colón.

▼ CAFÉ RIALTO *Cafe, Live Music*

☎ 96 394 08 77; Plaza del Ayuntamiento 17; ⏰ 8am-4pm Mon, 8am-11.30pm Tue-Fri, 4pm-midnight Sat & Sun; Ⓜ Xàtiva

An arty option that shares premises with Valencia's Filmoteca and Rialto theatre, this cafe is also a popular drop-in spot for literati throughout the day. There's live music at 11pm on Fridays.

▼ OCTUBRE *Cafe*

☎ 96 315 77 99; C de San Fernando 12; ⏰ 9am-9pm; 🚌 60, 81

Sip a quality coffee at the cafe of this fervently *valenciano* cultural centre, visit one of its temporary exhibitions or simply rest your feet after wandering around the nearby Mercado Central (p15).

★ PLAY

★ LA CLACA *Club*

☎ 669 32 50 79; www.laclaca.com, in Spanish; C de San Vicente Mártir 3; ⏰ 7pm-3.30am; 🚌 4, 70

Central and popular, La Claca has been in business for more than 25 years. It has a couple of dance floors where DJs play funk, hip-hop and indie, Tuesday to Sunday. Earmark Sunday evening, 8.30pm, for some of the best live flamenco in town.

>L'EIXAMPLE

L'Eixample (Ensanche in Spanish, meaning extension) grew fast in the 19th century as the rising middle classes sought modern, commodious residences that would fittingly express their new-found wealth.

Better-heeled Valencians head for L'Eixample for its exclusive shopping. In the crisscross of streets running roughly between C de Colón and Mercado de Colón are most of Valencia's swishest boutiques for clothing and accessories.

Also in this *barrio* are a pair of the city's finest Modernista buildings: Estación del Norte, work of art as much as transport hub, and the structurally splendid Mercado de Colón, freshly painted and primped, no longer the earthy market it once was, and not yet quite sure of its new role.

Latterly, L'Eixample has enjoyed a second surge of popularity, this time for its bars and restaurants. East side, west side of C del Conde de Altea, for example, just about every place is a restaurant or, in the odd gap, a congenial bar.

L'EIXAMPLE

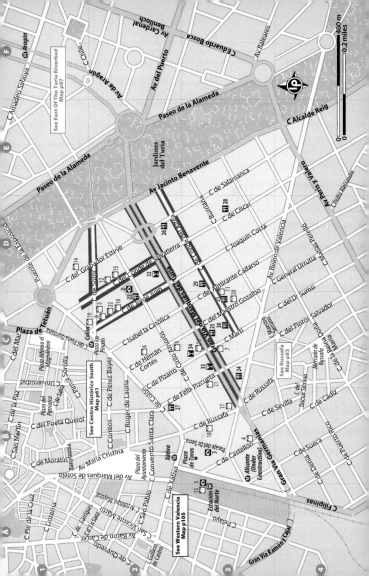

See East Of The Turia Riverbed
Map p97

See Centro Histórico South
Map p61

See Russafa
Map p83

See Western Valencia
Map p105

W Aragón
C Amadeo Saboya
Av de Aragón
Av Cardenal Benlloch
C Chile
C Eduardo Boscà
Av Baleares

Av del Puerto
Paseo de la Alameda
Paseo de la Alameda
C Alcalde Reig

Jardines del Turia
Av Jacinto Benavente
C de Salamanca
C de Ciscar
Av Peris y Valero
C de Buñol
28

Puente de la Exposición
C del Grabador Esteve
14
15
12
C del Conde de Salvatierra
C Joaquín Costa
Av Reino de Valencia
C Maestro Aguilar
26
27
C de la Reina Doña María

Plaza de Tetuán
Colón
19
C Poeta Querol
5
C de Jorge Juan
10
32
23
2
C de Jorge Juan
29
C del Almirante Cadarso
Av General Urrutia
C del Dr Sumsi
11
20

Plaza Alfonso el Magnánimo
C Isabel la Católica
C de Hernán Cortés
16
31
C de Colón
13
C del Maestro Gozalbo
30
25
6
C Martí
7
C Sorní
C del Pintor Salvador

C de Pérez Bayer
Universidad
C del Poeta Querol
C de la Paz
C San Martín
C de la Cruz
Pl de la Cruz
C de la Paz

C Correos
C Roger de Lauria
C de Pizarro
34
9
33
21
8
24
18
C de Russafa
C de Sevilla
C de Cádiz

C del Doctor Serrano
C Maestro Sanchis
Mercado de Russafa
Porta de la Mar
C del Dr Serrano

C de Félix Pizcueta
17
C de Castellón
3
4
Alicante (Under Construction)
Gran Vía Germanías
C de Sueca
C de Cádiz
C Pedro III El Grande
C Diana

Plaza del Ayuntamiento
Av del Marqués de Sotelo
Xàtiva
Plaza de Toros
Estación del Norte
13

Av María Cristina
Convento Santa Clara
Plaza de Xàtiva
C San Pablo
C de Xàtiva
C Pelayo
C Filipinas
Gran Vía Ramón y Cajal

C de Moratín
C Barcelonina
C de San Vicente Martir
C del Arzobispo Mayoral

C de Quevedo
Guillem de Castro
Av Barón de Cárcer
C de Quevedo
C Ciscar

N

0   400 m
0   0.2 miles

See Centro Histórico South
Map p61

◉ SEE

◉ ESTACIÓN DEL NORTE
C de Xàtiva; Ⓜ Xàtiva
Even if you're not taking the train, pass by Valencia's resplendent railway station (p22), soon to celebrate its first centenary.

◉ MERCADO DE COLÓN
☎ 96 337 11 01; C de Cirilo Amorós; ⏲ 8am-midnight; Ⓜ Colón
The soaring Mercado de Colón with its rich ceramic work outstrips the Mercado Central in its Modernista splendour. No longer a food market, alas, it's now occupied by boutiques, cafes and restaurants.

◉ MUSEO TAURINO
☎ 96 388 37 38; Pasaje del Dr Serra 10; admission free; ⏲ 10am-8pm Tue-Sun; Ⓜ Xàtiva
With images of macho men in figure-hugging sequinned suits and funny hats comes a collection of bullfighting memorabilia and a good 15-minute commentary-less video portraying a bull's life on the range up to its death in the ring. Afterwards, visit the adjacent bullring, strut in the sand of the central circle, and dream.

◫ SHOP

◫ ABANICOS CARBONELL
Arts & Crafts, Gifts & Souvenirs
☎ 96 341 53 95; www.abanicos carbonell.com; C de Castellón 21; ⏲ 9.30am-1.30pm & 4-8pm Mon-Fri; Ⓜ Xàtiva
For handmade fans with true cachet, visit this splendid little place, where the same family has been producing fans for five generations. Pick up a trim hand-painted item for around €20, buy one for as little as €1.50 (yes, truly) or invest up to €6000 for an antique work of art.

◫ ALEX VIDAL *Fashion*
☎ 96 342 73 37; www.alexvidal.es; C de Hernán Cortés 13; ⏲ 10am-1.30pm & 4-8pm Mon-Fri, 10am-2pm Sat; Ⓜ Xàtiva, Colón
Local designer Alex Vidal has his smart shop and headquarters here, selling women's haute couture, shoes and accessories that bear his own label, and also items from Italian brands that he's designed. Branches at C de Sorní 6 and in Centro Histórico South (p64). Also see the boxed text, p64.

THANKS FOR YOUR GOOD WISHES

In the main hall of Valencia's Estación del Norte, 'Bon voyage' is picked out in gold leaf in major languages, including Arabic and Chinese. 'Pleasant Journey' it quaintly wishes the anglophone traveller…

Beautiful handmade fans on display at Abanicos Carbonell

ALFREDO ESTEVE
Men's Clothing
☎ 96 374 08 38; Gran Vía del Marqués del Turia 18 & 32; ⏲ 10am-2pm & 5-8.30pm Mon-Sat; Ⓜ Xàtiva
Alfredo Esteve's two ultrasmart boutiques are the only places in Valencia where you'll find designer labels Gucci, Dior, Lanvin and Dolce & Gabbana for men: classic lines at No 18, sport- and leisurewear at No 32.

BAÑON
Accessories, Arts & Crafts
☎ 96 352 82 46; C de Jorge Juan 13; ⏲ 10am-9pm Mon-Sat; Ⓜ Colón

Bañon, an all-Valencian outfit, selects its wares from all over the world and peddles chic homeware, mock furs, kids' cuddly toys, watering cans and whatever else takes its fancy. There are three other branches around town.

BIMBA Y LOLA
Women's Clothing, Accessories
☎ 96 394 41 80; www.bimbaylola.com; C de Jorge Juan 17; ⏲ 10am-8.30pm Mon-Sat; Ⓜ Colón
This branch of a national chain, recently established on one of Valencia's prime shopping streets, flaunts boots, bags, bracelets,

smart sweaters, well-cut clothes and other gear to make you walk proud. There's another branch around the corner at C de Cirilo Amorós 44.

☎ BUENO PARA COMER
Delicatessen
☎ 96 316 11 46; www.buenoparacomer
.es, in Spanish; C del Almirante Cadarso
14; ☷ 10am-9pm Mon-Sat; ☐ 19, 40
Discerning expat Brits head for Good to Eat, with its attractive dark stained woodwork, to pick up Stilton, Caerphilly and other near-forgotten home pleasures. Its

wines (several available for tasting by the glass) and food from the five continents is selected by manager Dan Gill, latterly of Harrods' food hall in London.

☐ CACAO SAMPAKA
Chocolate & Sweets
☎ 96 353 40 62; www.cacaosampaka
.com; C del Conde de Salvatierra 19;
☷ 9am-9pm Mon-Sat; Ⓜ Colón
Here's a temple to cocoa and all that can be fashioned from it. Indulge yourself with a packet of handmade chocolates, all made from pure, unadulterated cocoa.

Be tempted by decadent delights at Cacao Sampaka

⌂ CORONEL TAPIOCCA
Fashion
☎ 96 352 78 50; www.coroneltapiocca
.com, in Spanish; Estación del Norte, C de
Xàtiva; ☾ 8am-9pm Mon-Sat, 10.30am-
noon & 5-8pm Sun; Ⓜ Xàtiva

In the main station shopping area, the Spanish chain Coronel Tapiocca (yes indeed, Colonel Tapioca, a figure that could come straight from a Tintin book) specialises in smart, casual outdoor clothing and equipment from the self-consciously retro to today's savannah specials.

⌂ ELVA *Accessories, Jewellery*
☎ 96 333 20 13; C del Grabador Esteve
15; ☾ 10am-2pm & 5-8.30pm Mon-Sat;
Ⓜ Colón

Elva Colomer herself collects and commissions the most stylish and tasteful of bags, berets, jewellery and other adornments that grace the sparse display cases around her walls. Pull out the drawers of her large central cabinet to reveal yet more wonders.

⌂ FRANCIS MONTESINOS
Fashion
☎ 96 394 06 12; www.francismontes
inos.com; C del Conde de Salvatierra 25;
☾ 10am-2pm & 5-8.30pm Mon-Sat;
Ⓜ Colón

Bright, sensual fabrics bedeck the window and a trio of chandeliers twinkle within the retail outlet of internationally acclaimed Francis Montesinos, doyen of Valencian fashion designers. The shop, which retails mainly women's haute couture, plus a few items for men, is a work of exuberant art in itself.

⌂ LINDA VUELA A RÍO
Fashion, Accessories
☎ 96 351 77 46; Gran Vía del Marqués
del Turia 31; ☾ 10am-2pm & 5-9pm
Mon-Sat; Ⓜ Colón

No name outside – far too flaunting – but the miniature statue of the Angel of Rió above the door of this tiny, street corner boutique gives a clue. Within are the finest in catwalk womenswear and accessories from Spanish and international fashion houses.

⌂ MANTEQUERÍAS VICENTE
CASTILLO *Delicatessen*
☎ 96 351 04 23; Gran Vía del Marqués
del Turia 1; ☾ 9am-2pm & 5-8.30pm
Mon-Sat; Ⓜ Xàtiva

Mantequerías, old-style specialist grocer shops, are gradually giving up in the face of supermarket competition. But not Vicente Castillo's, established in 1916, boasting Valencia's largest wine cellar with more than 12,000 bottles and offering the finest cheeses and sausages, and shelf upon shelf of tins and cans crammed with gastroexotica.

☐ MARTINEZ
Chocolate & Sweets
☎ 96 351 62 89; www.trufasmartinez
.com, in Spanish; C de Russafa 12;
🕑 9am-2pm & 4-8pm Mon-Fri, 9.30am-
2.30pm Sat; Ⓜ Xàtiva
Just smell the aroma of sweet
chocolate wafting through from
the rear oven! For more than 75
years, Martinez has perfected its
melt-in-the-mouth truffles, mar-
rons glacés and rich, dark handmade chocolates. The packaging is
almost as elegant as the treasures
within.

☐ NICHI SEIJO *Shoes*
☎ 96 350 93 67; C de Sorní 1;
🕑 10.30am-1.30pm & 5-8.30pm Mon-Sat;
Ⓜ Colón
Wooden floorboards and bare
brick walls; nothing, except for the
handsomest of wooden horses,
distracts your attention from the
fanciest of footwear on display at
this smart Valencian-owned shop.

☐ TOMÁS HUERTA
Delicatessen
☎ 96 395 80 09; www.alimentacion
tomashuerta.com, in Spanish; C del
Maestro Gozalbo 13; 🕑 9am-2pm &
5-8.30pm Mon-Sat; 🚌 19, 40
Established in 1916 by the present
owner's grandmother, this family-
owned delicatessen is a wonder
of aromas. Cavernous and clad
throughout in local tiles with

hams hanging from the ceiling
like porky chorus girls' thighs,
it's a treasure trove of cheeses,
sausages and other fine fare.

☐ TONUCA *Fashion, Accessories*
☎ 96 394 05 55; www.tonuca.com, in
Spanish; C de Félix Pizcueta 20; 🕑 10am-
2pm & 5-8.30pm Mon-Sat; Ⓜ Xàtiva
At her namesake boutique, prominent young *valenciana* designer
Tonuca Belloch sells her own
exciting creations, plus womenswear, bags and shoes fashioned
by select Spanish contemporaries.

☐ ZARA HOME *Homewares*
☎ 96 351 32 52; www.zarahome.com;
C de Jorge Juan 15; 🕑 10am-9pm Mon-
Sat; Ⓜ Xàtiva
Up-to-the-minute homewares
and kitchen tools from this smart
Spanish chain. See also p68.

🍴 EAT
🍴 ALTO DE COLÓN
Mediterranean €€€
☎ 96 353 09 00; www.elaltocatering
.com; Mercado de Colón, C de Jorge Juan
19; 🕑 lunch & dinner Mon-Fri, dinner
Sat; Ⓜ Colón
Up high within Mercado de Colón
the cuisine is subtle and imaginative, supplemented by a progres-
sion of small tasters. Lift your
eyes from the elegant all-white
decor and table linen to take in

the magnificent vaulted mosaic ceiling. Down at ground level, the related **Bamboo de Colón** (☎ 96 353 03 37) is larger, more informal and less pricey.

🍴 CHE *Basque* €
☎ 96 374 65 25; Av del Reino de Valencia 9; 🕐 lunch & dinner Tue-Fri, lunch Sat; 🚌 2, 19

This popular Basque place, more than 50 years in business, offers friendly service and excellent value (particularly the midday *menú* at €7.20). It's divided into intimate little booths and walls are plastered with photos, water-colours and whatever takes the owner's fancy.

🍴 FAST GOOD *Self-Service* €
☎ 96 374 84 07; www.fast-good.com, in Spanish; Gran Vía del Marqués del Turia 26; 🕐 10am-5pm & 8pm-midnight Mon-Fri, noon-5pm & 8pm-midnight Sat & Sun; Ⓜ Xàtiva

The pun on Fast Food doesn't quite work orally in English, but the intention's clear. Established by Catalan master chef Ferran Adrià, its fresh, contemporary de-sign and wholesome, well-priced food are a world away from your usual Bustgutburger joint.

Sleek self-service at Fast Good

🍴 FRESC CO *Self-Service* €

☎ 96 119 91 39; C de Salamanca 6; 🕑 12.30-5.30pm daily plus 8pm-midnight Fri & Sat; Ⓜ Colón; Ⓥ

You can lunch early or late at Fresc Co. The all-you-can eat under €10 buffet offers a veritable kitchen garden of salad items and a choice of pasta or pizza. With bare, mellow brickwork, it's an agreeable place to eat. Also at C de Felix Pizcueta 6 and in Centro Histórico South (p68).

🍴 JALASAN *Korean* €€

☎ 96 333 72 07; C de Ciscar 43; 🕑 lunch & dinner Wed-Sat, lunch Sun, dinner Tue; 🚌 13, 95

Myung Keun Lee not only serves authentic, tasty Korean food, he's also a gifted photographer. His haunting black and white photos bedeck the walls of this attractive, dark-wood place where classical music or jazz throbs softly in the background.

🍴 KERALA

Mediterranean Fusion €€

☎ 96 344 78 84; www.keralarestaurante.com, in Spanish; C del Conde de Altea 17; 🚌 19, 40

It's hard to be specific about the cuisine of Gabriele and his young team since their creative, excellent-value *menús* (lunch €13, dinner €22) change daily. Portions are plentiful and served with a smile.

🍴 LA GALLINETA

Mediterranean €€

☎ 96 336 36 64; www.gallineta.com, in Spanish; C del Conde de Altea 7; 🕑 lunch Mon & Tue, lunch & dinner Wed-Sat; 🚌 19, 40

Don't expect any concessions to slick design at this particularly friendly, spartan white-and-cream rectangle. All the energy goes into the innovative, quality cuisine, including a superb value midday *menú* (€14.50). For red wine, choose a bottle of smooth Casa de l'Ángel from the Valencia region's undervalued western flanks.

FREE FOR ALL

The following museums that normally charge admission are free to visitors on Saturday and Sunday:

Casa-Museo José Benlliure (p38)
Casa-Museo de Blasco Ibañez (p90)
L'Almoina (p49)
Museo de Historia de Valencia (p107)
Museo del Arroz (p91)
Museo Fallero (p99)
Museo Nacional de Cerámica (p62)

Other sites with free entry at weekends include:
Almudín (p48)
Cripta de la Cárcel de San Vicente Mártir (p49)
Las Atarazanas (p91)
Torres de Serranos (p40)

RIFF *Mediterranean*   €€€
☎ 96 333 53 53; www.restaurante-riff
.es, in Spanish; C del Conde de Altea 18;
⊗ lunch & dinner Tue-Sat; 🚌 19, 40
Riff, recently awarded its first
Michelin star, is as satisfyingly
spare in design as any Japanese
equivalent. Chef Bernd Knöller
prepares the finest Mediterranean
ingredients, supplemented with
delicate tidbits that keep rolling in.
Its lunchtime Menú Express (€29
and in fact agreeably leisured) is
great value. For €10 more, each of
its three courses comes accompa-
nied by a specially selected wine.

▼ DRINK

▼ AQUARIUM *Bar, Cafe*
☎ 96 351 00 40; Gran Vía del Marqués
del Turia 57; ⊗ 7am-1.30am; Ⓜ Colón
Aquarium, with its mirrors,
wooden panels and ultrapolite
waiters, sits in a time warp. But it's
arguably Valencia's best spot for
cocktails and quality tapas. If you
find the interior too stuffy, move
to the large summer terrace and
admire how the waiters weave

through the traffic, bearing your
drink.

▼ ISHAYA *Lounge Bar*
☎ 902 10 85 27; www.grupolasanimas
.com, in Spanish; Gran Vía del Marqués
del Turia 23; ⊗ 4pm-3.30am Mon-Sat;
Ⓜ Colón
Ishaya pulls in a mature, smoothly
attired yet still young-at-heart
clientele. Primarily a lounge bar,
elegant and Buddhist-themed,
it's agreeably exclusive. Fridays
are solely soul, with a few classic
tracks sneaking in.

▼ LAS ÁNIMAS *Music Bar*
☎ 902 10 85 27; www.grupolasanimas
.com, in Spanish; C de Pizarro 31;
⊗ 7pm-3.45am; 🚌 2, 41
All may seem antique at this spacious place with its revival 19th-
century wallpaper, grandmother's
toys and wooden angels gazing
down. But the music (DJ from midnight onwards) at this smart place,
a favourite of Valencia's beautiful
people, is eclectic and very much
of the moment.

>RUSSAFA

Up-and-coming Russafa has edge and, increasingly, style. Once known to the Arabs as the garden of Valencia, it has scarcely a blade of grass these days. Formerly popular and working class, the poorer neighbour of swanky, bourgeois L'Eixample, it's now a stimulating hybrid where ethnic shops and stores rub shoulders with designer chic.

Recovering an ancient identity, it counts many North Africans among its multiethnic mix of recent immigrants. Buildings and businesses are on a small scale: ethnic eateries and grocer's shops and stores stacked high with the cheap goods that forlorn sub-Saharans flog around town and along the beach.

But Russafa is also where artists and designers have established their studios and workshops. After dark, more and more people seeking night-time fun cross Av del Reino de Valencia (as significant a social dividing line as any railway track) to frequent its growing array of hip bars and trendy restaurants.

RUSSAFA

SEE

SHOP

EAT

DRINK

PLAY

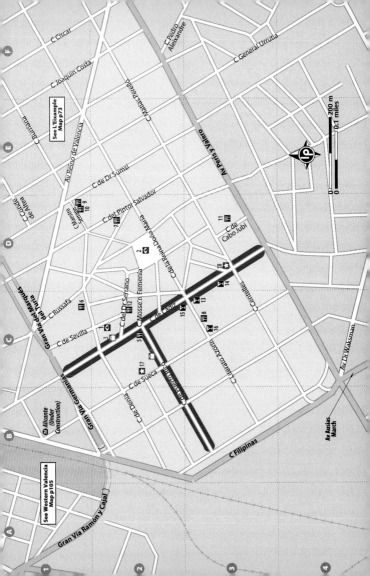

👁 SEE

👁 COLOR ELEFANTE

☎ 686 79 50 77; C de Sevilla 26; ⏰ usually 6-9pm Mon-Fri; 🚌 7, 19

This large, former industrial building is the workshop, gallery and cultural centre of sculptor Carles Albert Casanova. Cluttered and chaotic up on the 1st floor, its ground floor is the venue for quality temporary exhibitions.

👁 MERCADO DE RUSSAFA

C de la Reina Doña María; ⏰ 7.30am-2.30pm Mon-Sat; 🚌 7, 15

Unlike the architecturally stunning Mercado Central (p15) and Mercado de Colón (p74), Russafa's market belongs more to the silo school of concrete brutalism. But give it a chance – inside you'll find a popular market, well lit, its every booth still active and serving the neighbourhood.

🛍 SHOP

🛍 CAROLINE *Gifts & Souvenirs*

☎ 667 66 51 22; C de Cádiz 25; ⏰ noon-2pm & 5-9pm Mon-Sat; 🚌 2, 79

'Curiosity Shop' is how owner Juan Moragues describes his colourful boutique. It's packed with quirky, oddball gadgets, toys and fun items (an ashtray that's a fire bucket, another that carries a 'no smoking' sign) and also carries a cool range of designer T-shirts.

🎨 MIEL J REGAL *Arts & Crafts*

☎ 96 341 44 16; C de Puerto Rico 6; ⏰ 10am-2.30pm & 5.30-8pm Mon-Fri, 10am-2pm Sat; 🚌 2, 79

Juan-Jose Regal and, before him his father, have been selling honey, every drop from their own hives, for more than 50 years. And all else that bees produce – royal jelly, pollen, honeycombs and wax – measured out on a set of old needle weighing scales.

🍴 EAT

🍴 BASILICO
International, Fusion €€

☎ 96 316 83 69; C de Càdiz 42; ⏰ 1-11.30pm Tue-Sat, 11am-4pm Sun; 🚌 2, 79

An Anglo-Spanish couple run this excellent, tiny bar and restaurant. The menu, which changes according to what's in season, is eclectic, embracing, among others, dishes from China, India and Italy. There's a short, carefully selected wine list and service is friendly and informative.

🍴 BOCAMADA *Spanish* €€€

☎ 96 316 10 20; C de Denia 4; ⏰ lunch & dinner Mon-Sat; 🚌 2, 79

Owner Edmundo Ferrer is also an art collector and qualified sommelier – witness the engaging canvases around the walls and the selective wine list that changes with his menus, season by season. Food is

Jason Webster
British writer and long-term Russafa resident

What was it about Russafa that first brought you here? I ended up in Russafa because my wife (then my girlfriend) was living in this part of the city. I gave up a dead-end job in England and moved over to become a full-time writer in 2001. There was a friendly, villagelike feel to the area that soon made me feel at home, though it's become just a bit too gentrified for my liking in the past years. Something of the roughness and authenticity has been rubbed off. **What are your favourite outdoor places in Valencia?** The old riverbed is great for long, leisurely strolls. Valencia doesn't have many big open spaces, so it's a boon to have this long stretch of greenery. **Where in Valencia do you like to eat with friends?** Bodeguilla del Gato (p55; possibly the best tapas bar in town) and La Pepica (p93; for paella by the beach). **And your favourite bar?** It has to be Tula (p87), an emblematic Russafa coffee shop. **I understand that your latest work is a novel. Is it set in Valencia?** Yes, it's a crime novel called *Or The Bull Kills You*. My detective, Chief Inspector Cámara, lives here in Russafa.

ZUMOS
NATURALE

GRANIZADO DE
NARANJA
100% NATURAL

HORCHATA

BEBIDA ENERGÉTICA

very fresh (he flourished a carefully handled live lobster and bright-eyed sea bass to make his point to us) and portions are generous.

🍽 CASA BOTELLA
Mediterranean Fusion €€
☎ 654 84 93 33; C del Pintor Salvador Abril 28; 🕒 lunch & dinner Tue-Sat; 🚌 7, 19

At this friendly, intimate place, it's primarily rice dishes at midday and fusion in the evenings. Ask for Les Alcusses, a smooth red wine from the genial owner's home village. There's live jazz with dinner on Wednesdays.

🍽 LA FULOP *Fusion* €€€
☎ 96 333 03 70; C del Literato Azorín 7; 🕒 lunch & dinner Mon-Sat; 🚌 2, 79

With its minimalist, angular decor, all cubes and rectangles in olive, white and mulberry, La Fulop is a trendy, upmarket choice. Dishes are a delight to look at and consume, and the service is friendly. Pause too at its coolest of cool bars.

🍽 LA TORRIJA
Mediterranean Fusion €€
☎ 96 374 51 69; cnr C de Dr Sumsi & del Maestro Serrano; 🕒 lunch & dinner Mon-Sat; 🚌 19, 40

At this bright, welcoming offshoot of adjacent Michelin one-star restaurant, Torrijos, mains such as shoulder of lamb and meatballs

of bone marrow are served piping hot, the lids whisked off before you. Portions are small, exquisitely prepared and presented, and there's a good wine list.

🍽 MAIPI *Spanish* €€
☎ 96 373 57 09; C del Maestro Serrano 1; 🕒 lunch & dinner Mon-Fri; 🚌 19, 40

Gabi, the genial owner, is passionate about two things: the quality of his cuisine, all made with fresh ingredients from the nearby market, and Valencia football club, with signed photos of players past and present bedecking the walls. There's no menu and Gabi rattles off the dishes of the day with pride. This tiny, usually packed place is also excellent for tapas.

🍽 RESTAURANTE 18 *Fusion* €€
☎ 96 329 27 73; www.restaurante18 .com; C de Cabo Jubi 3; 🕒 lunch & dinner Tue-Sat; 🚌 6, 15

You can snack here pleasurably on pasta, sandwiches and tapas for around €10. But to really tease out the subtleties prepared by owner Ali and his team, put together your own three-course spread (€21) from its ample à la carte selection.

🍽 SORSI E MORSI
Italian €
☎ 96 322 55 43; www.sorsiemorsi.com; C del Dr Serrano 11; 🕒 lunch & dinner; 🚌 6, 19

Light, bright and decorated with cheery contemporary art, this very Italian option has an extensive list of piadinis and pastas. Go for the *cartoccio* (seafood and ropey noodles wrapped in tinfoil that's shaped into a swan). There's a second branch (p101) beside the City of Arts & Sciences.

▼ DRINK

▼ BACKSTAGE RUSSAFA *Bar*
☎ 96 334 89 13; C del Literato Azorín 1; ⏰ 7pm-1.30am; 🚌 2, 79

Backstage is popular with theatre folk and hangers-on – hence the name, decor and theatrical lighting. Big-band music throbs in the background, cocktails are shaken with histrionic panache and even the toilets are labelled (oh dear me, yes) *actores* and *actrices*.

▼ EL SOHO TERRACE *Bar*
☎ 678 79 80 76; C de Cádiz 70; ⏰ 5pm-1am; 🚌 7, 8

The team, like the clientele, are young at this welcoming spot. The usual minimalist interior with its white polka dots has charm, but what makes El Soho is its large rear terrace and stalwart olive tree – a rarity in built-up Russafa.

▼ TULA *Bar, Cafe*
☎ 96 341 50 95; www.tulacafe.es, in Spanish; cnr C de Cádiz & del Literato Azorín; ⏰ 9am-2am; 🚌 7, 8

Tula was among the very first of the spruce, modern Russafa bars. A friendly spot, it remains a relaxed, welcoming, laid-back place for a drink or snack, whether in the small, brightly coloured interior or on its terrace.

▼ UBIK CAFÉ *Bar, Cafe*
☎ 96 374 12 55; C del Literato Azorín 13; ⏰ 5-11pm Tue-Sat, 11am-11pm Sun; 🚌 2, 79

Ubik Café is a friendly cafe, bar and also bookshop (new titles on one side, secondhand the other). A comfy place to lounge and browse, it has a short, select list of wines and serves cheese and cold meat platters.

★ PLAY

★ CAFÉ MERCEDES JAZZ
Live Jazz
☎ 96 341 83 78; www.cafemercedes.es, in Spanish; C de Sueca 27; free-€15; ⏰ 10pm-3.30am Tue-Sun Oct-Jun, 10pm-3.30am Wed-Sat Jul-Sep; 🚌 7, 8

Here's yet another cultural activity that's planted its roots in the up-and-coming *barrio* (district) of Russafa. This attractive contemporary cafe attracts the best from the local jazz scene. Entry is free to all-comers jam sessions and very reasonable when a recognised combo's billed.

>BEACHES & THE PORT

The port area has changed radically in the last two decades. Abandoned maritime workshops and undistinguished houses were bulldozed to create the *paseo marítimo,* Valencia's promenade, stippled with bars and restaurants and extending for more than 3km beside the broad beaches of Las Arenas and La Malvarrosa.

More recently came the transformation of the inner harbour, previously commercial port, ferry departure point for the Balearic Islands and base of Valencia's fishing fleet. All were shifted outwards and southwards in order to transform the harbour for the America's Cup yacht races of 2007. Still fringed by the headquarters of the competing crews, the inner harbour has at its northern end a cluster of summertime-only fancy bars and restaurants.

To discover the port area's former soul, step back just one block to explore the narrow, grid-pattern streets of the old fisherfolk's quarter of El Cabanyal, these days threatened by a proposed new highway.

BEACHES & THE PORT

⊙ SEE
Casa-Museo Blasco
  Ibañez 1 B1
Casa-Museo de la
  Semana Santa
  Marinera 2 A5
Fountain Boat 3 B3
Las Atarazanas 4 A5
Museo del Arroz ....(see 2)
Veles e Vents 5 B5

⚡ DO
Catamaran Cruise
  Departures 6 B5

🍴 EAT
Barraca de Canyamelar .7 B4
Bodega Casa Montaña ...8 A4
Casa Guillermo 9 A4
La Pepica 10 C5
Lonja del Pescado 11 B3
Mar de Bamboo ....(see 5)
Tridente 12 C5

▼ DRINK
39° 27N 13 D5
Gandhara 14 B3
Vivir sin Dormir 15 C4

★ PLAY
Las Ánimas Puerto 16 B5
Mill Clubs 17 A5

◉ SEE

◉ CASA-MUSEO BLASCO IBAÑEZ

☎ 96 352 54 78 ext 2586; C de Isabel de Villena 159; €2; ⏱ 10am-2pm & 4.30-8.30pm Tue-Sat, 10am-3pm Sun; Ⓜ La Cadena

This elegant neoclassical building was the summer residence of Blasco Ibañez, Valencia's most famous literary son and author of, among many works, *The Four Horsemen of the Apocalypse*. Within are his work desk, the family piano and other furniture and photos of the period.

◉ CASA-MUSEO DE LA SEMANA SANTA MARINERA

☎ 96 352 54 78; cnr C del Rosario & Francisco Cubells; admission free; ⏱ 10am-2pm & 4.30pm-8.30pm Mon-Sat, 10am-3pm Sun; Ⓜ Francesc Cubells

For a flavour of the elaborate Semana Santa (Easter Week) processions that wind around the maritime district of El Cabanyal, visit this museum with its rich costume floats and regalia belonging

Exhibit at Casa-Museo de la Semana Santa Marinera

Museo del Arroz

to the participating Hermandades (Brotherhoods).

FOUNTAIN BOAT
Las Arenas; M Les Arenes
Here's an original piece of aquatic sculpture. Alongside the promenade, this otherwise ordinary piece of ironwork spurts water jets to make the shape of the hull and sails of a boat. Great idea – though in anything stronger than a light breeze, the sails disintegrate into formless cascades.

LAS ATARAZANAS
☎ 96 352 54 78 ext 4299; Plaza de Juan Antonio Benlliure; admission free; ☼ 10am-2pm & 4.30-8.30pm Tue-Sat; M Grau

Nowadays hosting temporary exhibitions, this vast building of mellow brick has the dimensions of a cathedral. But its original role was strictly secular; just a block back from the port and constructed in the 14th century, it functioned for centuries as a shipyard.

MUSEO DEL ARROZ
☎ 96 367 62 91; www.museoarrozvalencia.com, in Spanish; C del Rosario 1-3; €2; ☼ 10am-2pm & 4.30-8.30pm Tue-Sun, 10am-3pm Sun; M Francesc Cubells
Generators whirr, wheels creak, cogs turn and drive belts slap on the three floors of this splendidly reconditioned mill that processed rice from the fertile fields of the Albufera until the mid-1970s.

☉ VELES E VENTS

Port America's Cup; Ⓜ Neptú
Designed by British architect David Chipperfield and prized by fellow professionals, Sails and Winds is a simple, clean-lined four-storey structure in dazzling white concrete, constructed for the 2007 America's Cup. Nowadays roped off, forlorn and dead except in high summer, it has all the appeal of a multistorey car park.

🏃 DO

🏃 CATAMARAN CRUISE

☎ 96 381 60 66; www.mundomarino .es; Port America's Cup (below Veles e Vents); ☽ up to 4 times daily Tue-Sun; Ⓜ Neptú
A catamaran does a one-hour cruise around the harbour (€15). More romantic is its 1½-hour sunset trip (€20; 7.30pm or 8pm), taking in the harbour and a stretch of coastline and including a glass of Catalan bubbly. Reserve by phone or online.

🍴 EAT

🍴 BARRACA DE CANYAMELAR

Mediterranean €€
☎ 96 367 31 54; C de Barraca 40; ☽ lunch & dinner; Ⓜ Mediterrani
Four generations have brought gastronomic pleasure at this welcoming local favourite. Latest of the line, Miguel Ángel, still in

his twenties and having served his apprenticeship with a couple of local culinary maestros, prepares a magnificent-value five-course midday *menú* (€12), plus delicious rice and seafood creations.

🍴 BODEGA CASA MONTAÑA

Tapas €€
☎ 96 367 23 14; www.emilianobodega .com, in Spanish; C de José Benlliure 69; ☽ lunch & dinner Tue-Sat, lunch Sun; Ⓜ Mediterrani
Around since 1836 and famed for its varied tapas (just try the fresh anchovies), Bodega Montaña is a Valencian institution, with a marble bar, barrels and yellowing posters. Owner Emiliano Garcia, a qualified sommelier, serves excellent wines from bottle or barrel from his list of more than 1000 labels. Squeeze into the bar or phone to reserve a place in the small rear restaurant; menus are identical.

🍴 CASA GUILLERMO *Tapas* €

☎ 96 367 38 25; www.elreydelaanchoa .com; C de José Benlliure 26; ☽ 8.30am-3pm & 7-11.30pm Tue-Sat, 7-11.30pm Mon; Ⓜ Grau
Near Bodega Casa Montaña and a similar classic, clad in ancient post-ers and photos, Casa Guillermo has been around for more than 50 years. 'El Rey de la Anchoa', King of the Anchovies, it proclaims itself and anchovies (half/full portion

Bodega Casa Montaña

€12/20) are indeed the speciality. But it also does other wonderful pickled seafoods, very *valenciano* tapas and well-filled *bocadillos* (French-bread sandwiches). Reservations all but essential.

🍴 LA PEPICA *Fish, Rice* €€
☎ 96 371 03 66; www.la pepica.com; Paseo Neptuno 6-8; ⏰ lunch & dinner Mon-Sat, lunch Sun; Ⓜ Neptú
Larger and more expensive than its competitors, and renowned for its rice dishes and seafood, this is where Ernest Hemingway, among many other luminaries, once strutted. Browse the wall photos and tributes from prominent and less prominent clients.

🍴 LONJA DEL PESCADO *Fish* €
☎ 96 355 35 35; C de Eugenia Viñes 243; ⏰ dinner daily plus lunch Sat & Sun Mar-Oct, lunch & dinner Sat & Sun Nov-Feb; Ⓜ Eugenia Viñes
One block back from Malvarrosa beach, this busy, informal place in what's little more than an adorned tin shack offers unbeatable value

NEVER ON A MONDAY
Never's a tad too strong but Monday isn't the best day for fish dishes. The local fishing boats don't put out on Sundays so what's on the menu has been in the fridge over the weekend or comes fresh plucked from the deep freeze.

for fresh fish. Grab an order form as you enter and fill it in at your table.

🍴 MAR DE BAMBOO
Mediterranean €€

☎ 96 344 88 99; www.grupoelalto.com; Edificio Veles e Vents; ⌚ lunch & dinner Jul-Sep; Ⓜ Neptú

High-ceilinged, pure white and minimalist, summertime-only Mar de Bamboo occupies the ground floor of the Veles e Vents building. Stylish and spacious, it seems even larger thanks to its vast picture windows overlooking the port. Food is attractively presented and the rice dishes are particularly well prepared.

🍴 TRIDENTE
Mediterranean €€€

☎ 96 356 77 77; Paseo Neptuno 2; ⌚ lunch & dinner Tue-Sat, lunch Sun; Ⓜ Neptú

Sip an aperitif on the beachfront terrace of Tridente, the restaurant of Hotel Neptuno. Inside, there is an ample à la carte selection but you won't find details of the day's *menús* because they are delivered orally by the maître, who speaks good English. Dishes, with their combinations of colours and blending of sweet and savoury, are creative and delightfully presented, and portions are generous.

🍸 DRINK

🍸 39° 27N *Bar, Restaurant*

☎ 96 381 71 71; Marina Real Juan Carlos I; ⌚ noon-2am Mon-Sat, noon-8pm Sun; Ⓜ Neptú

Enjoy a drink or dine, inside or on the terrace, at this chic place perched atop the harbour wall. To one side are sweeping views of beach and shore, to the other, the port, while just below hopeful codgers sling a fishing line into the sea.

🍸 GANDHARA *Lounge Bar*

☎ 96 371 00 25; www.gandharaterraza .com, in Spanish; C de Eugenia Viñes 226; €12; ⌚ 11pm-4am Sun-Wed, 11pm-7am Fri & Sat May-Oct; Ⓜ La Marina

With its Buddhist statues, Hindu art, large gilded elephant and swathes of saris to break up the terrace into more intimate areas, Gandhara is perfect for relaxing on its low seating and floor cushions. There's also a small dance floor for those after something more vigorous.

🍸 VIVIR SIN DORMIR *Music Bar*

☎ 96 372 77 77; www.vivirsindormir .com, in Spanish; Paseo Neptuno 42; ⌚ 11am-4am; Ⓜ Neptú

Spacious 'Live without Sleep', with an ample terrace facing the sea, is wedged inside the long row of Las Arenas paella restaurants. Cafe by

Take in the fresh air and sea views at 39° 27N

day, it is very much music bar with its own resident DJ once night descends.

⭐ PLAY

⭐ LAS ÁNIMAS PUERTO *Club*

☎ 902 10 85 27; www.grupolasanimas .com; Edificio Docks, Paseo Neptuno; ☽ midnight-5am Sun-Tue, to 6.30am Wed-Sat Jun-Sep, midnight-6.30am Thu-Sat Oct-May; Ⓜ Neptú

A clunking metal staircase within this former warehouse leads you high to the two upstairs zones – one for danceable Spanish easy-pop, the other for quality electro and house. From 7.30pm until 3.30am, nonclubbers can relax

in its exotic lounge (daily) and open-air terrace (Wednesday to Saturday).

⭐ THE MILL CLUBS *Club*

www.themillclubs.com, in Spanish; cnr Av del Puerto & C del Padre Porta; around €8 (free to 3.30am); ☽ 2.30-7.30am Fri & Sat; Ⓜ Maritim-Serrería

In this megacomplex, you get three clubs in one, each with its own vast dance floor. The Factory churns out house and funk, in the Clubbing Room it's indie, pop and rock while Teatro Stage throbs to electro and techno. Your entry ticket lets you roam from one to another.

>EAST OF THE TURIA RIVERBED

The Ciudad de las Artes y las Ciencias is the defining feature of eastern Valencia. As you stand dwarfed beneath its spectacular, colossal structures, it's difficult to believe that barely a decade ago there was nothing here but sour, neglected riverbed.

Drawn by its presence, Valencia pushes more and more eastwards, towards the port and the Mediterranean, always an important part of her identity. High rises have sprung up, ranging from the architecturally stunning (how *do* the seemingly two-dimensional, apparently cardboard structures on the south bank manage to stay up?) to banal blocks.

To serve this new suburb, its residents and visitors, chic new restaurants and bars (swankiest of all, Terraza Umbracle, within the City of Arts & Sciences itself) look down upon the freshly landscaped riverbed.

To the north lies the university area with lots of longer-established bars, clubs and restaurants, from gourmet to great-value student haunts.

EAST OF THE TURIA RIVERBED

◉ SEE
Ciudad de las Artes y las
  Ciencias **1** C5
Gulliver **2** B4
Hemisfèric **3** C5
Jardín de Monforte **4** B2
Jardines del Real **5** B2
Museo de Bellas Artes ... **6** A2
Museo de las Ciencias
  Príncipe Felipe **7** C5
Museo Fallero **8** B5
Oceanogràfic **9** D5
Palau de les Arts
  Reina Sofía **10** C5

🏃 DO
Balneario
  La Alameda **11** B3

🛍 SHOP
Aqua **12** D5

🍴 EAT
La Drassana **13** C3
Les Maduixes **14** C3
Restaurante
  Submarino **15** D5
Samsha **16** C3
Sorsi e Morsi **17** C5
Tastem **18** C3
Vertical .... (see 12)

🍸 DRINK
Bla-Bla **19** D3
Café Alameda **20** B3
Café Valencia **21** B3

Manolo el del
  Bombo **22** B3
Mosquito **23** C3
On The Rocks **24** C3
Singles **25** C5
Terraza
  Umbracle **26** C5

⭐ PLAY
Albatros **27** C2
Babel **28** C3
Black Note **29** C3
Caribbean's **30** C3
Murray Club **31** D3
Palau de la
  Música **32** B4

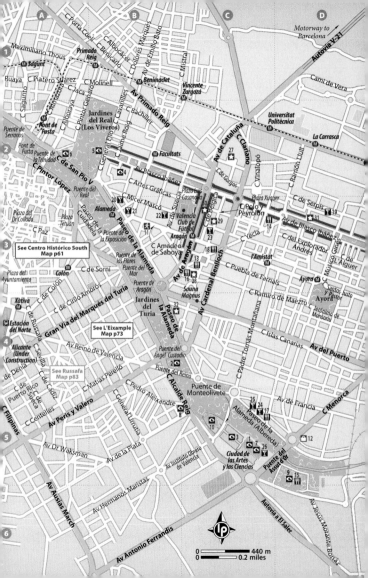

◉ SEE

◉ CIUDAD DE LAS ARTES Y LAS CIENCIAS

☎ 902 10 00 31; www.cac.es; Autovía a El Saler; Oceanogràfic €24, Hemisfèric €7.50, Museo de las Ciencias Príncipe Felipe €7.50, Oceanogràfic & Museo de las Ciencias Príncipe Felipe or Hemisfèric €26, all three €31.60; ◷ 10am-8/9pm mid-Jun–mid-Sep, 10am-6/8pm mid-Sep–mid-Jun; ◻ 35, 95
For details of this megacomplex that attracts more than four million visitors annually, see p10. Reserve online, by phone or through major hotels.

◉ GULLIVER

Jardines del Turia; admission free; ◷ 10am-8pm Sep-Jun, 10am-2pm & 5-9pm Jul & Aug; ◻ 19, 95
Lilliputian kids scramble, clamber and slide all over a magnificent, ever-patient Gulliver (gooly-*vare*) reclining in the riverbed. Nearby, there's minigolf, a conventional playground, skateboard ramp and giant chessboard.

◉ JARDÍN DE MONFORTE

C de Monforte; admission free; ◷ 10.30am-8pm Apr-Sep, to 6pm Oct-Mar; ◻ 9, 95
This haven of tranquillity, where languid Italianate statues pose between clipped knee-high boxwood hedges, is a favourite spot for bridal photos. There's no more pleasant place in town to munch your sandwiches or grab a quick nap.

◉ JARDINES DEL REAL

C de San Pío V; admission free; ◷ 7.30am-9.30pm Apr-Sep, to 8.30pm Oct-Mar; ◻ 9, 95
The Royal Gardens, more commonly called Los Viveros, reach down to the Jardines del Turia. Popular with Valencians, this is another lovely spot for a stroll and a drink at one of its cafe terraces.

CITY OF ARTS & SCIENCES

Packages
On weekends and school holidays, many hotels offer a package that includes accommodation and reduced-rate entry to the City of Arts & Sciences.

Avoiding the Oceanogràfic Queues
During school holidays, long ticket lines for the Oceanogràfic can build up. To save trouble and time if you haven't booked in advance, make the two-minute walk along to the Museo de las Ciencias Príncipe Felipe, where you can buy entry tickets for all City of Arts & Sciences attractions. Waiting time here is normally much shorter.

NEIGHBOURHOODS

EAST OF THE TURIA RIVERBED

◎ MUSEO DE BELLAS ARTES

☎ 96 387 03 00; C de San Pío V 9; admission free; 🕙 10am-8pm Tue-Sun; 🚍 79, 95

Valencia's spacious Fine Arts Museum ranks among Spain's best. See p20 for information.

◎ MUSEO FALLERO

☎ 96 352 54 78 ext 4625; Plaza de Monteolivete 4; €2; 🕙 10am-2pm & 4.30-8.30pm Tue-Sat, 10am-3pm Sun; 🚍 35, 95

Each Fallas (see p130), only one of the thousands of *ninots*, near-life-sized figurines that pose at the base of each *falla* (giant sculpture), is saved from the flames by

popular vote. It's sent here to rest, forever at peace.

◎ PALAU DE LES ARTS REINA SOFÍA

☎ 902 20 23 83; www.lesarts.com; Autovía a El Saler; 🚍 35, 95

Brooding over the riverbed like a giant beetle, its shell shimmering with translucent *trencadís* (slivers-of-broken-tile mosaic), is this stunning building, used primarily for opera and second only to Sydney's Opera House in capacity.

🏃 DO

🏃 BALNEARIO LA ALAMEDA

☎ 901 22 20 02; www.balneariola alameda.com; C de Amadeo de Saboya 14; €15; 🕙 9am-10pm Mon-Fri, 10am-9pm Sat & Sun; Ⓜ Alameda

From far beneath this spa, equipped with gym, sauna, massage rooms and a pool kept at 34°, warm, natural waters surge up from a depth of more than 650m.

Museo Fallero

🛍 SHOP
🛍 AQUA *Shopping Centre*
C de Luis García Berlanga 19-21;
🚌 **35, 95**

This new shopping centre is several cuts above the usual functional out-of-town boxes. Open lifts head skywards, escalators glide obliquely and bridges between each wing of its five floors are made of glass. Architecturally exciting, it's packed with national chains and local favourites.

🍴 EAT
🍴 LA DRASSANA
Mediterranean €€

☎ **96 369 24 84; C de Antonio Suarez 29;**
🕑 **lunch & dinner Wed-Sat, lunch only Mon & Tue;** Ⓜ **Aragón**

Rafael Ballester offers subtle tapas and a mains menu that changes with the seasons. With room for only 26, the cool decor of cream and light-beige makes this place appear much larger. And a welcome touch, rare in Spain: wines are at shop prices plus a reasonable €5 corkage fee.

🍴 LES MADUIXES
Vegetarian €€

☎ **96 369 45 96; C de Daoiz y Velarde 4;** 🕑 **lunch Mon-Sat, dinner Thu-Sat;** Ⓜ **l'Amistat;** Ⓥ

With her son and daughter, Mariña Canera runs the Strawberries,

nearly 25 years in business and a top vegetarian choice. There's an excellent value, four-course lunchtime *menú* (€12) and all sorbets and ice creams (try the chestnut) are homemade. Wines too are special: some organic, all from small, independent producers.

🍴 RESTAURANTE SUBMARINO
Mediterranean €€€

☎ **96 197 55 65; Camino de las Moreras;**
🕑 **lunch & dinner;** 🚌 **35, 95**

This elegant circular restaurant, its broad, glowing lamps like giant lilypads, is within the Oceanogràfic (p10). Instead of wallpaper, more than 1000 silvery bream slowly gyrate. If you feel uncomfortable eating fish as those unblinking eyes stare reproachfully, there are meat alternatives…

🍴 SAMSHA
Mediterranean Fusion €€

☎ **96 389 19 02; C del Periodista Ros Belda 4;** 🕑 **lunch & dinner Tue-Sat, lunch Sun;** Ⓜ **Aragón**

Samsha's hip red, green and mauve colours and clean lines are matched by the equally inventive, technicolour cuisine of up-and-coming young chef Víctor Rodrigo. He manages, among his other talents, to offer 17 different kinds of bread to match the 17 items on the menu.

¶ SORSI E MORSI
Italian €€

☎ 96 381 17 20; Paseo de la Alameda 44;
🕐 lunch & dinner; 🚌 35, 95

Chic sister to the hip Italian trattoria of the same name in Russafa (p86), it offers the same menu with the same delightful pasta dishes, piadini and lipsmacking desserts.

¶ TASTEM *Japanese*
€€

☎ 96 369 68 51; www.tastem.com, in Spanish; C de Ernesto Ferrer 14; 🕐 lunch & dinner Tue-Sat, dinner Sun; Ⓜ Aragón

Tastem is designed with great contemporary flair by a young *valenciano* who has spent many years in Japan. The decor, all beige and soft greys, is positively soothing, as a pair of Japanese chefs chop and mould the subtlest of dishes behind the long counter.

¶ VERTICAL *International* €€€

☎ 96 330 38 00; www.restaurante vertical.com, in Spanish; top fl, Hotel Confortel 4, C de Luis García Berlanga 19; 🕐 lunch & dinner Mon-Sat; 🚌 35, 95

This Michelin one-star restaurant has a staggering panorama comprising the sea, the port and the City of Arts & Sciences. Organised on two levels (choose, paradoxically, the lower one to obtain the best views), it offers a single gourmet *menú* described (in English) at your table. Dishes (count on four entrées, a main dish and two desserts) are small and exquisite.

▾ DRINK

▾ BLA-BLA *Bar, Cafe*

☎ 96 355 50 55; www.cafeblabla.com, in Spanish; C de Serpis 62; 🕐 4pm-1.30am; Ⓜ La Carrasca

Bla-Bla, with its plush red drapery and mirrors, is perfect for a relaxing drink. Candles flicker, a soft, yellow light plays, there's a particularly well stocked bar and staff are friendly and affable. There's an entrance on Plaza de Honduras.

Try Tastem for fine Japanese cuisine

☿ CAFÉ ALAMEDA *Bar, Cafe*

www.cafealameda.com, in Spanish; Paseo de la Alameda 6; ☏ **3pm-3am Mon-Fri, noon-3am Sat & Sun;** Ⓜ **Alameda**

At this pleasant, boho bar and cafe, you sit on simple wooden chairs or slatted benches that could have been borrowed from a park. Art exhibitions change monthly, live jazz trills every Tuesday from 7.30pm and there's a large outdoor terrace.

☿ CAFÉ VALENCIA *Bar, Cafe*

☎ **96 369 32 62; Paseo de la Alameda 14;** ☏ **8.30am-midnight Mon-Wed, 8.30am-4am Thu-Sun;** Ⓜ **Alameda**

On summer days, sit outside on the terrace. Inside, two bars flank the parquet flooring. From it, chairs are pushed back at 11pm on the dot, Thursday to Sunday, as Café Valencia morphs into a *discoteca*.

☿ MANOLO EL DEL BOMBO *Bar*

☎ **610 20 44 09; www.manoloeldel bombo.com, in Spanish; Plaza del Valencia Club de Fútbol 5;** ☏ **noon-10pm Tue-Sun;** Ⓜ **Aragón**

You'll already know Manolo if you've watched the Spanish national football team on TV. With a beret bigger than a dinner plate, he thumps his bass drum – there it is, dangling from the ceiling – to rouse the fans. A place of pilgrimage for serious footy fans, his bar is plastered with photos and mementoes.

☿ MOSQUITO *Music Bar*

C de Polo y Peyrolón 11; Ⓜ **Aragón**

DJs at this tiny box of a place dispense classic soul, R&B, and a leavening of hip-hop. However many shots you knock back, you'll know you're in the right place by the giant papier mâché mosquito hovering above its circular bar.

CINEMA & MUSIC

In the university area, a couple of great multiscreen independent cinemas show undubbed films, while Valencia's prime venues for music and opera overlook the riverbed.

Albatros (☎ 96 393 26 77; www.cinesalbatrosbabel.com, in Spanish; Plaza Fray Luis Colomer 4; Ⓜ Universitat Politécnica)

Babel (☎ 96 362 67 95; www.cinesalbatrosbabel.com, in Spanish; C Vicente Sancho Tello 10; Ⓜ Aragón) Sister to Albatros, offers the same adventurous programming for cinephiles.

Palau de la Música (☎ 96 337 50 20; www.palaudevalencia.com; Paseo de la Alameda 30; Ⓜ Alameda) Hosts mainly classical music recitals.

Palau de les Arts Reina Sofía (☎ 902 20 23 83; www.lesarts.com; Autovía a El Saler) See p10 and p99.

▼ ON THE ROCKS *Cocktail Bar*
☎ 96 381 43 30; www.valenciaonthe rocks.com, in Spanish; Paseo de la Alameda 45; ☾ noon-3.30am; 🚌 35, 95
It surely has to be a G&T infused with blue Bombay Sapphire gin if you choose the open area, clad in blue, that overlooks the Hemisfèric. Within, sip a stylish cocktail (check the vast selection of spirits behind the bar) beneath dangling polystyrene rocks.

▼ SINGLES *Cocktail Bar*
☎ 96 330 59 75; Paseo de la Alameda 43; ☾ noon-1.30am; 🚌 35, 95
Within the baroque interior of this cool place, patronised in the main by smart 30-somethings, are three well-stocked bars. It's worth visiting for the decor and crowd, despite the hit-and-miss service.

▼ TERRAZA UMBRACLE
Lounge Bar, Club
☎ 96 331 97 45; www.umbracleterraza .com, in Spanish; City of Arts & Sciences, Autovía a El Saler; ☾ midnight-6.30am Thu-Sat mid-May–mid-Oct; 🚌 35, 95
At the southern end of the Umbracle walkway within the City of Arts & Sciences, here's a cool, sophisticated spot to spend a hot summer night. Catch the evening breeze under the stars on the terrace, then drop below to MYA (☾ 1-7.30am Fri & Sat year round), a top-of-the-line club

with an awesome sound system. Admission (€20 including first drink) covers both venues.

★ PLAY

★ BLACK NOTE *Live Jazz*
☎ 96 393 36 63; C de Polo y Peyrolón 15; ☾ 10pm-3am Mon-Sat; Ⓜ Aragón
Valencia's most active jazz venue has live music Monday to Thursday (with an all-comers jam session on Monday). On Friday and Saturday, there's good canned blues, soul and jazz. Admission, including your first drink, costs from €6 to €15 depending on who's grooving.

★ CARIBBEAN'S *Club*
C de Bélgica 5; ☾ Tue-Sat; Ⓜ Aragón
Drinks (try the mojitos) are decently priced at this small, below-ground and usually jam-packed dance bar that blends house, hip-hop and R&B. Wednesday night is student night.

★ MURRAY CLUB *Club*
☎ 96 371 65 96; Av de Blasco Ibáñez 111; €10; ☾ 1-7am Wed-Sat; Ⓜ La Carrasca
Choose your night to match your music: Wednesday is normally hip-hop with R&B, on Thursday it's indie and rock while the weekend is for indie too with plenty of techno as well. There's a live band most Fridays.

>WESTERN VALENCIA

At the western limit of the former Río Turia riverbed, a wonderful green stripe that coils through the city, is Bioparc, equally green, a particularly ecofriendly animal park and the city's newest major attraction. Beside Bioparc stretches the recently landscaped Parque de la Cabecera with its lake, dry stone walls replicating the field divisions of the interior and, in this flattest of cities, a hillock – albeit a manmade one – that's worth the easy walk up for a special panorama of Valencia.

After dark, the area around Mercado de Abastos, Valencia's former wholesale market – and in particular C de Juan Llorens – has a cluster of flamboyant music bars. Here in the west too are some of the city's major clubs and discotecas.

WESTERN VALENCIA

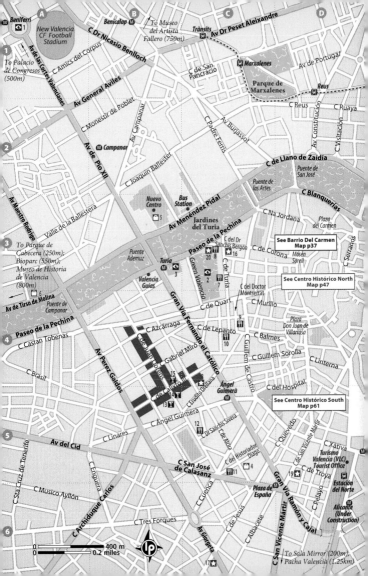

V

NEIGHBOURHOODS

WESTERN VALENCIA

◉ SEE

◉ BIOPARC

☎ 902 25 03 40; www.bioparcvalencia
.es, in Spanish; Av de Pio Baroja 3; €21;
🕐 10am-dusk; Ⓜ Nou d'Octubre; ♿
Forget zoos and menageries:
Valencia's latest major attraction,
where wild animals apparently
(fear not: only apparently) roam
free, is a hugely ecosensitive,
warmly recommended enterprise.
There's also a restaurant (*menú*
adult/child €12.50/6.50). For
details, see p17.

◉ DAMA IBÉRICA

Av de las Cortes Valencianas; Ⓜ Beniferri
This striking head-and-shoulders
creation rises 20m high above a
busy roundabout. It's made up of
22,000 small, cobalt-blue ceramic
tiles, each in the form of a diminu-
tive lady. The whole recalls the
classic Iberian statue of the Dama
de Elche, unofficial symbol of the
Valencia region.

◉ JARDÍN BOTÁNICO

☎ 96 315 68 00; C de Quart 80; €1;
🕐 10am-dusk Tue-Sun; Ⓜ Turia

Jardín Botánico

BEST OF THE BRIDGES

As many as 18 bridges span the former Turia riverbed. Appropriately, both the furthest west, Puente Nueve de Octubre, and the newest and furthest east, Puente del Assut d'Or (2008), were constructed by Valencia's most famous contemporary son, Santiago Calatrava (see p147). Other impressive ones include:

> Puente del Reino – Guarded by magnificent bronze gargoyles.
> Puente del Mar – Mellow late-16th-century stonework and exclusively pedestrian.
> Puente de las Flores – The Bridge of Flowers (2002), packed with fresh blooms.
> Puente de la Exposición – Popularly known as La Peineta (the hair comb), Calatrava's first creation for the city.
> Puente de la Trinidad – 16th-century and the city's oldest.
> Puente de Serranos – Valencia's second oldest, former gateway to the north.

Established in 1802 and nowadays administered by the University of Valencia, these were Spain's first botanical gardens. With mature trees and plants, an extensive cactus garden and a lovely restored 19th-century shade house, it's a tranquil place to relax.

◐ JARDÍN DE LOS HESPÉRIDES

Paseo de la Pechina; admission free; ⏱ **10am-8pm Apr-Sep, to 6pm Oct-Mar;** Ⓜ **Turia**

Abutting the Jardín Botánico, this prize-winning modern garden could not be more remote in style. Shorter on green space, it has the formality of a classic French garden with cypress trees, low banks of herbs and staggered terraces where tangy citrus trees flourish.

◐ MUSEO DE HISTORIA DE VALENCIA

☎ **96 370 11 05; C de Valencia 42; €2;** ⏱ **10am-2pm & 4.30-8.30pm Tue-Sat, 10am-3pm Sun;** Ⓜ **Nou d'Octubre**

Charting Valencia's past, this interactive museum, with film and video, occupies a vast, cathedral-like building of glazed brick that was once a municipal water cistern. Borrow the museum's informative English-language folder and, to stay in historical sequence, follow the numbered panels – not always easy and you'll need to cast around.

◐ MUSEO DEL ARTISTA FALLERO

☎ **96 347 96 23; www.gremiodeartistas falleros.com, in Spanish; C del Ninot 24; €2.50;** ⏱ **10am-2pm & 4-7pm Mon-Fri, 10am-2pm Sat;** 🚌 **12, 28**

Run by the guild of Falla artists, its centrepiece, a huge *falla* (giant sculpture erected in the streets during the Las Fallas festival) under construction, gives a good idea of how these giants are designed and erected. Crowding the corridors are more than one hundred *ninots* (near-life-sized figurines that strut and pose at the base of each *falla*) as well as smaller, winsome *fallas* for children.

PALACIO DE CONGRESOS
☎ 96 317 94 00; www.palcongres-vlc .com; Av de las Cortes Valencianas; Ⓜ Palau de Congresos

The Palacio de Congresos with its slender columns, shimmering aluminium and trowel-shaped roof, will simply take your breath away. Nicknamed the *pez varado* (beached fish), it was designed by British architect Sir Norman Foster.

PARQUE DE CABECERA
Paseo de la Pechina; admission free; Ⓜ Nou d'Octubre

Landscaped and recovered from what was until recently a seedy, unkempt area of the riverbed, this public park has a small lake where you can hire swan-shaped pedalos. Climb the hillock, for all the world like a Mesapotamian zigurrat, if you want to obtain a great view of the riverbed and the city.

SHOP
BODEGA BEAL'S *Wines*
☎ 96 385 52 49; C de Alcira 15; Ⓨ 9am-1.45pm & 5-8.30pm Mon-Sat; Ⓜ Plaza de España

Cross to the Gran Vía's less fashionable side to explore this wonderful specialist shop. It carries a huge range of spirits as well as aisle upon aisle of wines, nudging 2000 different bottles, from palatable and costing less than €4 to sky's-the-limit finest vintages.

DISCOS AMSTERDAM *Music*
☎ 96 348 39 65; www.discosamsterdam .tk, in Spanish; Local 80, Lower Level, Centro Comercial el Nuevo Centro, Av de Pío XII 2; Ⓨ 10am-9pm Mon-Sat; Ⓜ Turia

Juan Vitoria, author, journalist and broadcaster, started this magnificent music shop more than 25 years ago. Plastered with posters, it specialises in indie titles and the seriously retro and rare. It will undertake searches and accepts email orders worldwide. It's opposite the fashion shop Zara, on the lower level of the Nuevo Centro shopping centre.

MERCADO DE FUENCARRAL *Shopping Centre*
☎ 96 317 36 40; www.mdf.es, in Spanish; Av de Tirso de Molina 16; Ⓜ Turia

This swanky, recently opened ultramodern shopping centre has all the usual and many unusual suspects, including Pepita, sister to Pepita Pulgarcita (p43) and, among other eating opportunities, a cool cafe run by Opera Prima (p54). See p112 for places to drink in the centre.

🍴 EAT

🍴 ANA EVA *Vegetarian* €€
☎ 96 391 53 69; C de Turia 49; 🕑 lunch & dinner Thu-Sun; Ⓜ Turia; Ⓥ

The smartest of Valencia's limited vegetarian options has tasteful decor and a delightful rear patio. It prepares some very imaginative dishes and does great juices. With starters including rice, pasta, potatoes and couscous, you won't walk out rumbling.

🍴 DUKALA
Moroccan €€
☎ 96 392 62 53; C del Dr Sanchis Bergón 29; 🕑 lunch & dinner Fri-Sun, dinner Wed & Thu; Ⓜ Turia

Dukala (du-*ka*-la) is hyperfriendly, intimate (reservations are essential) and bedecked with striped Moroccan fabric. Noreddine prepares the best Maghrabi cuisine in town, including the tastiest bread rolls. Order a pot of the mint tea, poured from a height, or choose from the small, carefully selected wine list.

🍴 EL PEIX DAURAT
Mediterranean Fusion €€
☎ 635 41 34 76; www.elpeixdaurat .com, in Spanish; C del Dr Montserrat 14; 🕑 dinner Mon-Sat; Ⓜ Ángel Guimerà

The pleasant young team cook in full view of the diners. The menu is creative and portions are generous, enhanced by sauces, subtle combinations and spices (there's an Asian tang to many of the dishes).

🍴 LES NÍTS *Mediterranean* €€
☎ 96 391 63 40; www.lesnits.com, in Spanish; cnr C de Lepanto & Botánico; 🕑 lunch & dinner Tue-Sat; Ⓜ Ángel Guimerà

Intimate with minimalist decor, the Nights offers a splendid five-course *menú* (€25) and tantalizing à la carte choices. Portions don't spill over the edge of the plate but the quality is excellent and the imaginative desserts are to die for.

🍴 MEY MEY *Chinese* €€
☎ 96 384 07 47; www.mey-mey.com; C del Historiador Diago 19; 🕑 lunch & dinner; Ⓜ Plaza de España

The circular pool and low, wooden ceiling exude positive feng shui at this superb Cantonese restaurant. Nibble delicate dim sum, followed by the *fantasía mandarín* (shrimps, mixed meats and vegetables in an edible, crispy basket) or indulge in the magnificent seven-course *menú de degustación*.

NEIGHBOURHOODS

WESTERN VALENCIA

▮ VILLAPLANA *Tapas* €€
☎ 96 385 06 13; www.restaurante
villaplana.com, in Spanish; cnr C de Buen
Orden & Dr Sanchis Sivera 24; ⏱ 7.30am–
midnight Mon-Sat; Ⓜ Ángel Guimerà
Even though this long-established
Valencian favourite can accom-
modate more than 300 (how is
a mystery since you never feel
overcrowded), it's wise to reserve
for dinner. 'We specialise in everything,' says its tongue-in-cheek
visiting card and, indeed, the
range of tapas on offer is huge.

▼ DRINK
▼ CAFÉ CARIOCA *Music Bar*
☎ 96 384 50 51; www.cafe-carioca.com,
in Spanish; C de Juan Lloréns 52; ⏱ 5pm-
3.30am; Ⓜ Ángel Guimera

Cave-like with funky mosaic walls
where tiny silver figurines glisten,
Café Carioca has three bars. The
tempo of the music increases as
the night wears on (expect dance,
hip-hop, soul and house), there's
plenty of dancing and a live Brazil-
ian combo performs from 2.30am
on Wednesday.

▼ PEATONAL *Music Bar*
☎ 617 08 95 32; C de Juan Lloréns 39;
⏱ 6pm-3.30am Tue-Sat; Ⓜ Ángel
Guimera
Peatonal, like Café Carioca just opposite, is a long-established stayer
in a zone where bars come and go.
The music's disco, mainly Spanish
pop and commercial, and there's a
DJ on Thursday. Drinks are two for
the price of one until 1am.

Villaplana

This favourite night-time tipple, served by the jug, couldn't be further from humble H20. Bar staff squeeze a handful of oranges, toss in whatever spirits take their fancy and top up the jug with cava, Spain's Champagne-method bubbly from Catalonia.

ⓨ TANGO Y TRUCO *Bar*
☎ 96 385 18 37; www.tangoytruco.net, in Spanish; C de Calixto III 10; ⏰ 5pm-1.30am Mon-Sat, from 9.30am Sun; Ⓜ Ángel Guimera

Posters and photos of Maradona, Eva Perón and other icons, Argentinian and international, plaster the walls of this cosy corner of Buenos Aires in downtown Valencia, with an intellectual, left-wing clientele. Clashing with the intimacy is its giant TV screen for music and live football.

⭐ PLAY
⭐ CAFÉ DEL DUENDE
Flamenco
☎ 630 45 52 89; www.cafedelduende .com; C de Turia 62; ⏰ Wed-Sat 10pm-2.30/3.30am; Ⓜ Turia

Café del Duende, more Andalucian than *valenciano*, offers quality live, authentic flamenco on Thursdays and Fridays at 11.30pm and the best of recorded flamenco whenever it's open. The place is a small sweatbox so arrive early to claim a seat.

⭐ DUB CLUB *Club*
C de Jesús 91; free to €10; ⏰ 10pm-6am Thu-Sun; Ⓜ Jesús

'We play music not noise' is the slogan of this funky dive with its long, narrow bar giving onto a packed dance floor. And it does offer great music and great variety including live jazz jamming, reggae, dub, drum 'n' bass, funk, breakbeat and more.

⭐ EL LOCO *Live Music*
☎ 96 391 41 51; www.lococlub.org, in Spanish; C de Erudito Orellana 12; €8-15; ⏰ 10.30pm-3.30am Wed-Sat; Ⓜ Ángel Guimerà

Hugely popular despite being a bit off the beaten beat track, it's strictly live at El Loco. This long-established venue puts on groups and solo acts, both Spanish and from beyond the frontiers.

⭐ LA INDIANA *Club*
☎ 96 384 50 51; www.laindiana.com, in Spanish; C de San Vicente Mártir 95; €12-20; ⏰ midnight-7am Thu-Sat Sep-Jun; Ⓜ Plaza de España

La Indiana pulls in a lively crowd, drawn by the hip new decor and about the best sound system in town. Lights, lasers and video screens too are equally top of the range. It's mainly funk and house on the ground floor and strictly Latino upstairs.

★ MERCADO DE FUENCARRAL *Lounge Bar, Cafe*

☎ 96 317 36 40; www.mdf.es, in Spanish; C de Tirso de Molina 16; Ⓜ Turia

Among the drinking and snacking options within this trendy new shopping centre (p108) are Sofá-Club with its long bar, giant entertainment screens and regular live events and PRPGND (short for propaganda – don't ask us why!), less frenetic and with a large terrace overlooking the riverbed. Pepita has an extensive wine list, DJs and sometimes live music while at Laydown, yes, you can indeed squat or stretch out as you dine or sip a cocktail.

★ PACHA VALENCIA*Club*

☎ 609 64 35 46; www.pachavalencia. com, in Spanish; C de San Vicente Mártir 305; €20; ⏱ midnight-7am Thu-Sat Sep–mid-Jun; 🚌 27

One of a fistful of spinoffs worldwide from the legendary Ibiza club, Valencia's Pacha, with its sumptuous decor, has a vast main floor playing mainly house and with space for 1200 dancers to fling themselves around. Its Pacha-

chá plays commercial music and can pack in up to 500, and there's a cool VIP area, where the studiously beautiful can look down on the masses.

★ SALA MIRROR *Club*

☎ 607 65 97 05; www.discomirror.es, in Spanish; C de San Vicente Mártir 200; €15; ⏱ midnight-8am Thu-Sat Sep-Jun; Ⓜ Jesús

This vast club seems to change names every couple of years or so. Constantly popular whatever it calls itself, its two areas normally heave with clubbers and it keeps its capacity to pull in top-of-the-bill live acts.

★ TEATRO DE MARIONETAS LA ESTRELLA *Theatre*

☎ 96 356 22 92; www.teatrolaestrella .com, in Spanish; Sala la Petxina, C del Dr Sanchis Bergón 29; €8; ⏱ 6.30pm Sat & Sun Sep-Jun; Ⓜ Turia

For more than 30 years Gabriel Fariza and Maite Miralles have been making their own puppets and sets, writing their own material, touring internationally and delighting both children and adults. It's a family favourite so do book in advance.

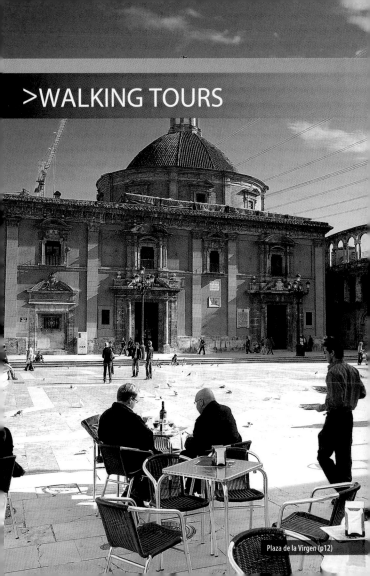

>WALKING TOURS

Plaza de la Virgen (p12)

HIGHLIGHTS OF THE CENTRO HISTÓRICO

This whistlestop walk takes you past the historic quarter's major monuments. It could easily take a whole day if you explore each one.

From **Plaza de la Virgen** (**1**; p12) head briefly west along C de Caballeros, the main thoroughfare of medieval Valencia. Turn right into C de Serranos. At **Torres de Serranos** (**2**; p40) go left and follow C de Roteros for **Iglesia del Carmen** (**3**) and **Palacio de Pineda** (**4**) on **Plaza del Carmen** (**5**; p39). Turn left (south) into C Pintor Fillol, which becomes C Baja (Low St), another important medieval thoroughfare.

At **Plaza del Tossal** (**6**), pause for a drink in **Sant Jaume** (**7**; p45) then continue down C de Bolsería. Turn left into Plaza del Mercado to visit the **Mercado Central** (**8**; p15) and **La Lonja** (**9**; p18).

Bear right at the junction with C de San Vicente Mártir to see the **Town Hall** (**10**; p62) and **Main Post Office** (**11**; p62) in **Plaza del Ayuntamiento** (**12**; p62). Returning, head north up C de San Vicente Mártir to **Plaza de la Reina** (**13**), and slip up the lane that runs left (west) of the cathedral to rejoin your starting point.

distance 2.5km **duration** 45 minutes

▶ **start** Plaza de la Virgen

● **end** Plaza de la Virgen

MODERNISMO MEANDER

This walk takes in Valencia's main Modernista (art nouveau) buildings.

After sniffing around **Mercado Central** (**1**; p15), take in the elaborate stucco facade of **C Ramilletes 1 (2)**, on the corner where C Ramilletes meets Plaza del Mercado. Follow Av María Cristina to Plaza del Ayuntamiento, site of the resplendent **Main Post Office** (**3**; p62).

At the end of C Ribera, detour briefly to **Estación del Norte** (**4**; p22). Take C de Russafa, then turn left for **Casa Ortega** (**5**; Gran Vía del Marqués del Turia 9) with its elaborate floral decoration. Go left along C de Félix Pizcueta, then first right, stopping at **Casa Ferrer** (**6**; C de Cirilo Amorós 29), garlanded with stucco roses and ceramic tiling. Continue northwards to **Mercado de Colón** (**7**; p74), a good spot for a drink, then head northwest to **Casa del Dragón** (**8**; C de Jorge Juan 3), named for its dragon motifs.

Cross C de Colón and head northwards for C de la Paz. Both **Hotel Vincci Palace** (**9**) and **No 31 (10)** have elaborate, decorated *miradores* (corner balconies), while **Red Nest Hostel (11)** has delicate, leafy iron railings.

At the end of C de la Paz, continue straight – maybe calling in for an *horchata* at **Horchatería Santa Catalina (12**; p59) – to return to Mercado Central.

distance 3.25km **duration** 1 hour

▶ **start** Mercado Central 🚌 7, 81

● **end** Mercado Central 🚌 7, 81

GREEN VALENCIA

Within this busy city, you can hop from park to park, garden to garden, following the Jardines del Turia along the old riverbed.

Begin with the formal charm of **Jardín de Monforte** (**1**; p98). Exiting, go right (north), then left along Av Blasco Ibañez and enter the **Jardines del Real** (**2**; p98). After 75m, turn left beside two large **bird cages** (**3**). Exit by the park's main southern gate and take the short foot tunnel to **Jardines del Turia** (**4**; p19). Turn right, upstream, passing the **Torres de Serranos** (**5**; p40), a baseball diamond and **rugby pitch** (**6**), following the riverbed under five bridges. Sip a drink at the small **cafe** (**7**) in the riverbed, below the bus station. Cross to the southern bank and climb the stone ramp (once used to roll logs for the sawmills of the Barrio del Carmen).

Before you is **Jardín de los Hespérides** (**8**; p106) but you'll have to double back 150m to cross Paseo de la Pechina at the traffic lights. After visiting the gardens, continue southwards, then go left briefly at C de Quart to enter the **Jardín Botánico** (**9**; p106).

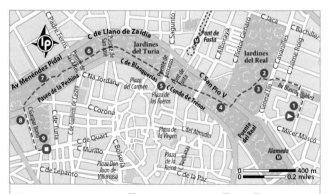

distance 3.5km **duration** 1 hour ▶ **start** Jardín de Monforte ⊟ 9, 95 ● **end** Jardín Botánico Ⓜ Turia

>DAY TRIPS

A sailing boat drifts silently through La Albufera (p119)

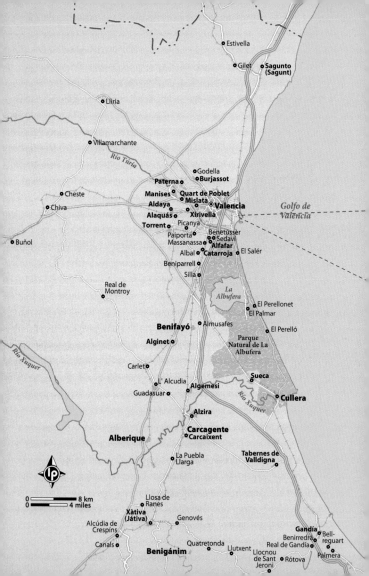

LA ALBUFERA

For an open air day out, visit La Albufera, a huge freshwater lagoon 10km south of Valencia. Have a paella lunch and boat trip and linger until sunset.

A mere puddle compared to its former vastness, the Albufera, which expands and contracts according to season, now averages 2837 hectares, having dwindled because of human activity, in the main the leeching of water for rice cultivation. It's a breeding ground and sanctuary for both migrating and indigenous birds; 90 species regularly nest around its reedy shores while more than 250 others use the Albufera as a staging post on their migrations. Between lake and sea is **La Devesa**, a narrow, protected strip of ancient sand dunes, anchored by pine trees, that's a delight to roam.

The **Racó de l'Olla Visitors Centre** (☎ 96 162 73 45; ⏰ 9am-2pm year-round plus 4-5.30pm Tue-Thu Oct-May) has a birdwatching hide, observation tower and exhibitions on both the lake and rice cultivation. Ask for its informative booklet in English.

Surrounded by rice paddies, La Albufera lays claim to be the very birthplace of paella. At the lake's southern limit, in the village of **El Palmar**, which was once an island, every second house seems to be a restaurant – and indeed there are more than 25 of them, compared with a resident population of around 900. Most are run by ex- or part-time fisherfolk, who harvest fish and eels from the shallow – scarcely 1m-deep – waters, and specialise in paella, other rice and seafood dishes and *all i pebre*, eels hauled wriggling from the lake and simmered in a garlic-rich peppery stew. The fare and prices are much the same, whichever restaurant you choose. For added value, select one that has a picture window overlooking the lake or paddy fields.

After lunch, take a trip on the lagoon in a *barquet*, a special flat-bottomed boat. As you drift, look out for *barracas*, typical Albufera houses with their steeply pitched, gabled, thatched roofs.

INFORMATION

Location Around 10km south of Valencia.
Getting There Valencia Bus Turistic (☎ 96 341 44 00; www.valenciabusturistic.com) offers a multilingual two-hour tour (€14) including a half-hour boat trip. **Autocares Herca** (☎ 96 349 12 50; www.autocaresherca.com) has at least five buses daily to El Palmar.
Eating A rice-based lunch at any of El Palmar's many restaurants.

SAGUNTO

You come to Sagunto (*valenciano:* Sagunt) primarily to enjoy the spectacular panorama of the town, coast and green sea of orange groves from its hilltop fortress complex. Here up high, rambling through the tangle of cacti and chaos of shaped stones, you can sense the loneliness of soldiers over centuries, drafted to this lonely eyrie to watch over the plain below.

Nowadays a sleepy spot, Sagunto was a thriving Iberian community (called – infelicitously, with hindsight – Arse) as early as the 5th century BC, minting its own coins and trading with both Greeks and Phoenicians. In 219 BC Hannibal, on the epic journey that led him and his elephants over the Alps towards Rome, besieged the town for eight months. Rather than capitulate, the inhabitants chose mass suicide and their town was razed, sparking the Second Punic War between Carthage and Rome. Rome won, named the town Saguntum and set about rebuilding it.

From the train station it's a 10-minute walk to the tourist office. A further 15-minute uphill walk through narrow streets (detour briefly into the **Judería**, the former Jewish quarter) brings you to the 1st-century **Roman theatre**. Its modern restoration – more wholesale construction – is controversial but the acoustics remain outstanding and it's the main venue for Sagunto's three-week, open-air **arts festival** in August.

Higher up, the rambling **fortress complex** (admission free; 🕐 10am-dusk Tue-Sat, 10am-2pm Sun), mostly in ruins, was constructed, modified and added to over centuries. The seven sections each speak of a different period in Sagunto's long history. Girdling the hillside for almost a kilometre, its highlights include the well-preserved Plaza de Armas, left (east) of the main entrance, and, beyond it, the massive Muslim gateway of the Plaza de Almenara. There's also a small Antiquarium Epigráfico, a collection of mainly Roman inscriptions on stone.

INFORMATION

Location 25km north of Valencia.
Getting There Half an hour from Valencia by frequent train. AVSA (☎ 96 267 14 16) buses run every half hour from Valencia's bus station.
Contact Tourist Office (☎ 96 266 22 13; www.aytosagunto.es/turismo, in Spanish; Plaza del Cronista Chabret)
When to Go Avoid high summer around midday – the castle complex hasn't a blade of shade.

LA TOMATINA

Buñol? It'll make you see red.

On the last or penultimate Wednesday in August (the date varies), an estimated 50,000 people take part in Spain's messiest and most bizarre festival. La Tomatina, creation of Buñol, an otherwise drab industrial town about 40km west of Valencia city, is a tomato-throwing orgy.

The festival's origins, though relatively recent, are obscure, but who cares? Just before noon on this very red-letter day, truckloads of ripe, squishy tomatoes (more than 100 tonnes of them) are tipped out to the waiting crowd and everyone joins in a frenzied, cheerful, anarchic tomato battle, while locals play hoses and throw buckets of water on the seething, increasingly red mass below until, promptly at 1pm, an explosion signals the end of proceedings.

DAY TRIPS

XÀTIVA

Xàtiva makes an easy and rewarding day trip from Valencia. It has a small historic quarter and a mighty castle strung along the crest of the Serra Vernissa, at whose base the town snuggles.

The Muslims established Europe's first paper manufacturing plant in Xàtiva. It later enjoyed fame as the birthplace of 17th-century artist José de Ribera and the Borgia Popes, Calixtus III and his nephew Alexander VI. The town's glory days ended in 1707 when Felipe V's troops rampaged through the town in the War of Succession.

Breathtaking views from the castle at Xàtiva

What's of interest lies south and uphill from the Alameda, the town's wide, shady main avenue. Drop into the tourist office there to pick up its free English guide, *Xàtiva: Monumental Town*.

In the days before piped town water, Xàtiva used to proclaim itself 'The City of a Thousand Fountains' and indeed many houses had their own water supply. The abundant spring Bellús spurts almost 10km away and still feeds the town's splashing fountains.

Noble mansions flank C Ángel, which becomes C Moncada, while parallel C Corretjería has more modest but equally attractive bourgeois residences. On the penultimate floor of **Museo del Almudín** (☎ 96 227 65 97; C Corretgería 46; €2.10; ☉ 9.30am-2.30pm Tue-Fri, 10am-2.30pm Sat & Sun mid-Jun–mid-Sep, 10am-2pm & 4-6pm Tue-Fri, 10am-2pm Sat & Sun mid-Sep–mid-Jun), the upside down portrait of Felipe V isn't an oversight of the cleaning staff: it hangs that way in retribution for the monarch's torching of the town. Outside the 16th-century **Colegiata Basílica** (Collegiate Church; ☉ 10.30am-1pm) are a couple of fine statues of Xàtiva's two Borgia popes.

It's a long haul up to the **castle** (€2.10; ☉ 10am-6pm/7pm Tue-Sun), from where the views are sensational. On the way up, on your left is the 18th-century **Ermita de San José** and, to the right, the lovely Romanesque **Iglesia de Sant Feliu** (1269), Xàtiva's oldest church. Alternatively, hop aboard the little tourist train (€4 return) that heads up from the tourist office at 12.30pm and 5.30pm (4.30pm November to March) or call a **taxi** (☎ 96 227 16 81) and stride back down.

If you've brought a picnic, enjoy it in the castle grounds, lording it over the plain below. For gourmet cuisine, drop into **Hostería Mont Sant** (☎ 96 227 50 81; www.mont-sant.com) as you walk down the road from the castle. Set charmingly amid extensive groves of palm and orange, the hotel runs a splendid restaurant, divided into intimate crannies.

INFORMATION
Location 60km southwest of Valencia.
Getting There By regional train (40 minutes, half-hourly). Most Madrid-bound express trains stop in Xàtiva too.
Contact Tourist Office (☎ 96 227 33 46; www.xativa.es, in Spanish; Alameda Jaime I 50) On Xàtiva's shady main avenue.

In this chapter, we've drawn together in discrete sections some of the main sights and activities that may have brought you to Valencia — such as its food and restaurants, the best shopping areas, our favourite bars, clubs and art galleries, plus places around town that are especially suitable for children.

An impressive selection of wine and tapas at Pepita Pulgarcita (p43)

ACCOMMODATION

Impelled by a surge in overseas visitors since the millennium, Valencia is especially well endowed with cheerful, great-value backpacker hostels. At the other end of the spectrum and boosted by the 2007 America's Cup yachting jamboree, the city now boasts half a dozen five-star hotels. In between, there's ample choice for all budgets.

There are three main areas for hotels. In the Centro Histórico you're well placed for restaurants and nightlife. You'll also be able to walk to most of the main sites and all the shopping areas that matter. If the City of Arts & Sciences is your main destination, there is a fistful of new hotels for most budgets nearby. Then again, you may prefer to make the beach your focus (plenty of nightlife down there too, in summer), choosing one of the sleeping options near the shore and either travelling into the heart of town by bus or tram or setting aside a modest element of your budget for taxis.

Hotel tariffs vary hugely (by as much as 200%) according to season, especially in midrange and top-end hotels that cater primarily to business travellers. Hostel rates are much more constant.

Tip-top hotel rates apply only for about four weeks each year – times when it will be difficult to get a room anywhere and when reservations are essential. Maximum tariffs apply for major national holidays such as Semana Santa (Easter Week) and between 11 and 19 March, when Valencia celebrates Las Fallas, Spain's wildest street party. The city is also a popular convention and trade fair venue, so maximum rates apply too for major commercial fairs, such as the Feria del Mueble (Furniture Fair) in September.

On weekdays, most guests staying at top-end and midrange hotels are from the business community. One happy consequence for short-break travellers is that weekend rates (usually Friday, Saturday and Sunday) are often considerably cheaper than the normal tariff. Check whether breakfast is thrown in for free as well.

Many hotels, particularly those near the City of Arts & Sciences, offer tempting weekend packages that include accommodation, optional meals and entry to attractions of the Ciudad de las Artes y las Ciencias. In an effort to attract the family trade, several offer weekend deals where children under 12 sleep for free.

Hotel rates throughout the month of August (July too in some cases), when everyone's down at the coast, are also often at their lowest.

One last point, especially if you're reserving by phone. Non-Spanish visitors sometimes complain that the hotel booking they made has not been honoured to the letter. But often it's a question of linguistic confusion rather than inefficiency. If you book a double room *(habitación doble)*, you'll probably be allocated one with twin beds, something that can present a challenge to those on an amorous outing. If you want to snuggle together, be sure to specify a double bed *(cama matrimonial)* when you reserve.

BEST BOUTIQUE HOTELS
> Hospes Palau de la Mar (www.hos
pes.es)
> Petit Palace Bristol (www.hthoteles
.com)
> Hotel Ad Hoc (www.adhochoteles
.com)
> Chill Art Hotel Jardín Botánico (www
.hoteljardinbotanico.com)
> Hotel Inglés
(www.hotelinglesvalencia.com)

BEST BUDGET CHOICES
> Hôme Backpackers (www.likeathome
.net)
> Hilux (www.feetuphostels.com)
> Center Valencia (www.center
-valencia.com)
> Indigo Youth Hostel (www.indigo
hostel.com)

> Red Nest Hostel (www.nesthostels
valencia.com)

BEST SHORT LET APARTMENTS
> Accommodation-Valencia.com (www
.accommodation-valencia.com)
> Rôôms de Luxe (www.roomsdeluxe
.com)
> 40flats.com (www.40flats.com)
> 50flats.com (www.50flats.com)

BEST FOR THE BEACH
> Room Mate Marina Atarazanas (www
.room-matehotels.com)
> Neptuno (www.hotelneptuno
valencia.com)
> Las Arenas (www.hotel-lasarenas
.com)
> El Coso (www.hotelelcoso.com)

EATING AROUND

Valencia is the capital of *la huerta,* a fertile coastal agricultural plain that supplies the city with delightfully fresh fruit and vegetables (see them piled high in the Mercado Central). It's a fishing port as well, so the bounty of the sea also comes direct and fresh to your restaurant table.

Rice is the staple of much Valencian cuisine – and the basis of paella, the dish that Valencia exported to the world. Eating for *valencianos* is, especially at weekends, a convivial, drawn-out affair. And few activities are more sociable than lunching with friends or family, scooping your paella from a common pan at one of the many Las Arenas beachside restaurants. Ask for your paella *de carne* (with chicken, rabbit and perhaps a handful of snails) or *de marisco* (with seafood).

It would be a pity, though, to restrict yourself to paella. Valencia is rich in restaurants that specialise in other rice dishes such as *arroz a banda* (rice simmered in a fish stock), *arroz negro* (rice with squid, simmered in its own ink) and *arroz al horno* (oven-baked rice). One other very Valencian favourite, *arròs amb fesols i naps* (rice with haricot beans and turnips), is several times tastier than its ingredients might suggest. Rice dishes are often served with a pot of *all i oli,* a very garlicky mayonnaise. And if you reach the point when you just can't face another grain, try another local variant, *fideuá* (pronounced *fee-day-WA*), where small noodles replace the rice.

Two other regional favourites to look for on menus are *all i pebre,* chunks of eel from La Albufera simmered in a peppery sauce, and *escarrat,* strips of salted cod and roasted red pepper bathed in olive oil. And just about every restaurant menu will offer *ensalada valenciana,* a salad of lettuce, tomato, onion, olives, tinned tuna and, sometimes, hardboiled egg.

As Valencia becomes increasingly international, so its range of eating options widens. A smart, minimalist new restaurant seems to spring up almost monthly, particularly around L'Eixample, the up-and-coming area for diners. Sometimes the quality of the cuisine is at variance with the smart decor, but we've every confidence in the ones we've selected.

The influx of immigrants from South America over the last decade has led to the opening of Argentinian (mmm, such beef!), Peruvian and Colombian restaurants that cater as much to *valencianos* (not by nature all that gastronomically adventurous) as to their own communities.

Valencia isn't big on flesh-free options (we once followed a vegetarian cookery course at a hotel training school in town where they simply picked out the meaty lumps and called what was left a vegetarian stock). This said, just about every restaurant in town can toss a decent salad and you'll never go hungry when there's a tortilla behind the bar. See below for our list of the best veggie options in town.

Lastly, let's not overlook the tapa, that quintessentially Spanish dish that can be everything from quick snack to an element of a full meal. In addition to the tapas bars and restaurants that we recommend on p136, try Tasca Ángel (p58) for its sardines and Bar Pilar (p55) for its mussels in broth.

From Monday to Friday, nearly all restaurants offer a *menú del día* at lunchtime. This three-course special may or may not include coffee, wine or both. Whatever the category of the restaurant, the *menú* is normally an excellent deal, and lets you sample the cuisine of places that might otherwise be above your usual budgetary limit.

BEST LUNCHTIME BARGAINS
> L'Hamadriada (p43)
> Mattilda (p43)
> Pati Pineda (p43)
> Kerala (p80)
> La Gallineta (p80)

BEST VEGETARIAN
> Les Maduixes (p100)
> Espaivisor (p56)
> La Tastaolletes (p42)
> La Lluna (p42)
> Ana Eva (p109)

BEST ETHNIC
> Dukala (Moroccan; p109)
> Jalasan (Korean; p80)
> Tastem (Japanese; p101)
> Mey Mey (Chinese; p109)
> Sorsi e Morsi (Italian; p86)

BEST OF THE BEST
> La Sucursal (p42)
> Alto de Colón (p78)
> Riff (p81)
> Vertical (p101)
> Tridente (p94)

Top left A feast of fresh produce at Mercado Central (p15)

LAS FALLAS

Las Fallas (15 to 19 March), Europe's largest and longest street party, is an exuberant, anarchic, round-the-clock swirl of fireworks, music, explosions and fire that brings an estimated two million visitors to the city. This wild fiesta honours San José (St Joseph), father of Jesus. It recalls the time, says tradition, when carpenters' apprentices, once spring was in the air, burnt winter's accumulated cut-offs to honour their patron, the Greatest Carpenter of All.

The more than 350 *fallas* are giant sculptures of papier-mâché and, increasingly, environmentally harmful polystyrene. The most expensive in 2009 cost €900,000 (oh yes, we've got those euro zeros right!). Grotesque, colourful and kitsch, they satirise celebrities, current affairs and local customs.

Around-the-clock festivities include street parties, paella-cooking competitions, parades, open-air concerts, bullfights and free fireworks displays. Then, in the *cremà,* after midnight on 19 March, every single *falla* goes up in flames – except for one small *ninot* (near-life-sized figurine that strut and pose at the base of each *falla*), elected by popular vote and saved for display in the city's Museo Fallero (p99).

The bald statistics from Fallas 2009 give an idea of the scale of the partying: total *fallas* construction costs were €10,645,280; there were 300 firefighters on duty for the *cremà;* the largest fireworks display exploded 4280kg of gunpowder and was watched by half a million spectators. On the upside, the festival brought an estimated extra revenue of €750 million for Valencia. On the downside, 7500 tonnes of rubbish was collected and 84 pickpockets arrested.

For more about Las Fallas, visit www.fallasfromvalencia.com, the English-language website of the official Junta Fallera, the organising body, or visit www.fallas.com, its main site with an English option.

SHOPPING

For fashion, Valencia's annual Pasarela del Carmen collection can't rival the catwalks of Barcelona or Madrid. Even so, there's some pretty slinky stuff to be searched out, whether in the shops of the most prominent designers, around the upbeat boutiques or within the trendiest of national chains.

The Centro Histórico abounds in small, independent boutiques touting clothing and accessories for him and her. At weekends and sale time you'll have to elbow your way along C de Colón, Valencia's main shopping street. Always busy, it's flanked on either side by smart branches of Spanish chains, where prices are still markedly lower than elsewhere in Europe. To its south, along the intersecting grid pattern streets of L'Eixample (in particular C de Salvatierra, Jorge Juan and Sorní) are smart, exclusive designer shops. Northwards, along C del Poeta Querol, pan-European brands such as Hermés, Louis Vuitton, Loewe and Bulgari feature, together with Valencia's very own Lladró (p65).

As in any other large Spanish city, there's no shortage of behemoth shopping centres in and around town. Two that stand out from the usual are Mercado de Fuencarral (p108), relatively small and boutique in style, and Aqua (p100), gleaming glass, towering high and Valencia's newest.

BEST DELICATESSENS
> Bueno Para Comer (p76)
> Opera Prima (p54)
> Añadas de España (p64)
> Navarro (p66)
> Tomás Huerta (p78)

BEST FOR FASHION
> Tonuca (p78)
> Retal Reciclaje Creativo (p54)
> Linda Vuela a Río (p77)
> Alex Vidal (p74)
> Francis Montesinos (p77)

BEST BOUTIQUES
> Monki (p54)
> Madame Bugalú (p53)
> Caroline (p84)
> Hakuna Matata (p53)
> Cactus (p52)

SMARTEST SPANISH CHAINS
> Purificación García (p66)
> Massimo Dutti (p66)
> Mango (p66)
> Zara (p68)
> Armand Basi (p64)

OPEN AIR VALENCIA

Valencia's trump summertime card is its beach, wide and more than 3km long. Despite the cranes and commercial port to the south, it's clean. It's raked daily in season for the smallest bottle top or lolly stick. With easy access by bus or high-speed tram, it's a great resource on the city's doorstep.

Thanks to the farsightedness of earlier generations, Valencia also has more than its share of formal gardens and parks. Jardines del Real, or Viveros, was once palace grounds, later the municipal nursery and is nowadays a lovely green urban space with a glorious rose garden at its heart. Right next door is the more intimate Jardín de Monforte (pictured below), also in its time the gardens of a fine mansion. Jardín Botánico, Spain's oldest botanical garden, is still a university research area and charges a token euro to keep the riffraff out. Its upstart new neighbour is the Jardín de los Hespérides, modern and as formally laid out as any of its classical predecessors.

Finally, less structured and more varied, the Jardines del Turia, all nine snaking kilometres of them, are at once playground, safe urban thoroughfare, cycleway and sportsground; a wonderful free resource for all.

BEST GARDENS & PARKS
> Jardín de Monforte (p98)
> Jardines del Real (p98)
> Jardín de los Hespérides (p107)
> Jardín Botánico (p106)
> Parque de Cabecera (p108)

BEST OTHER OPEN SPACES
> Bioparc (p17)
> Jardines del Turia (p19)
> Paseo Marítimo (p88)
> Las Arenas and La Malvarrosa beaches (p88)

BARS & CLUBS

Fuelled by a large student population, Valencia has one of Spain's best nightlife scenes. It cranks up late; most bars and pubs begin to fill around 10pm but the majority of dance clubs don't deign to open their doors until around midnight.

The Barrio del Carmen, with both the grungiest and grooviest collection of bars, has the best vibes. In the universities area, on and around Av Aragón and Av Blasco Ibañez, bars and dance clubs swarm with students. The streets east of Gran Vía Marqués del Turia and extending into Russafa are an up-and-coming area. Those around the Mercado de Abastos attract a predominantly younger set, while the port is the place for late-night clubbing at weekends.

Opening times may change to reflect new hours determined by the local government. At the time of writing, many bars with terraces stay open until 1.30am, the permitted maximum. Music bars and many others continue until 3.30am, their own limit. Clubs generally rock from Thursday to Saturday and tend to close between 6am and 8am.

If you're warming up in a music bar and intent on late-night clubbing, look out for club flyers that entitle you to free or discounted entry.

BEST CAFES & CULTURE
> Café de La Nau (p71)
> Octubre (p71)
> Café Rialto (p71)
> Café Alameda (p102)
> L'Ermitá (p44)
> Ubik Café (p87)

BEST BARS FOR MUSIC
> Jimmy Glass (p44)
> Turmix (p45)
> Las Ánimas (p81)
> Mosquito (p102)
> Café Carioca (p110)

BEST PLACES TO CHILL OUT
> Terraza Umbracle (p103)
> Café de las Horas (p58)
> Gandhara (p94)
> Zumería Naturalia (p59)
> Chill Out (p44)

BEST CLUBS
> Las Ánimas Puerto (p95)
> Radio City (p59)
> The Mill Clubs (p95)
> La Indiana (p111)
> Café Mercedes Jazz (p87)

CONTEMPORARY ART GALLERIES

Valencia is a relatively small city by pan-European standards. All the same, it manages to sustain more than 30 contemporary art galleries (one memorable Friday evening, we were invited to no less than *eight* first nights). Some are small, some more substantial, some confined to local artists and others enjoying international reputations. These private galleries display the best of recent Spanish and European art. Focussing upon emerging talents, they complement the rich offerings of IVAM (p38) and, on a much more modest but sometimes equally stunning scale, the Palacio Joan de Valeriola (p50).

Conveniently, most of these private galleries fall inside the Centro Histórico, so you can visit them during an easy walk within its bounds (for details of each, including opening hours, see the boxed text, p69). Elsewhere, stretch your legs just a little more to browse the streets of Russafa, where you'll stumble across the studios and workshops of the yet-to-become famous.

For a complete list that includes an explicit map, pick up the free pamphlet *Valencia Arte Contemporánea*. Updated every two months, it's available from tourist offices, many art galleries and quite a few major hotels. Admission to all is free and everything exhibited is for sale.

If you're planning to home in on one particular gallery, it's worthwhile ringing up in advance, just in case it happens to be between exhibitions.

Galeria La Nave (p69)

VALENCIA FOR CHILDREN

Should sightseeing pall, Valencia has plenty of outdoor fun for children. Take the high-speed tram to the long strip of beach at Las Arenas with its bouncy climbing frames, shallow waters and grainy sand (the ideal texture for complex castle construction). Or descend to the greenness of the former riverbed with plenty of informal romping space, punctuated by playgrounds.

But there's no reason why sightseeing should induce the dreaded 'I'm bored' syndrome. At the western limit of the riverbed, Bioparc (p17) is a wonderful ecofriendly animal park. Make a day of it at this end of town by exploring Museo de Historia de Valencia (p107), then taking a trip on the swan-shaped pedalos in Parque de Cabecera (p108).

At the other extremity, in the City of Arts & Sciences, the Hemisfèric Imax cinema and the Oceanogràfic are fun for all ages, while the Museo de las Ciencias Príncipe Felipe, well signed in English, will stimulate the over-10s.

If you're in town over the weekend, the Teatro de Marionetas La Estrella (p112) puts on great, supremely visual puppet shows, even if the language washes over you.

If the city's beginning to close in, head southwards a little. Follow a lunchtime paella in El Palmar with a boat trip on the Albufera lake (p119), then explore this reedy, watery environment's visitors centre with its viewing tower and bird hide. Alternatively, the rambling fortress and Roman theatre at Sagunto (p120) are great for playing soldiers (but mind those prickly pears!).

FUN FOR ALMOST FREE

> Gulliver (p98) and the Jardines del Turia (p19)
> Las Arenas and La Malvarrosa beaches (p88)
> Jardines del Real (p98)
> Chasing pigeons in Plaza de la Virgen (p12)
> The high speed tram (p150)

TO SHARE WITH MUM & DAD

> Bioparc (p17)
> The Oceanogràfic (p10)
> A carriage ride (p51)
> A catamaran cruise (p92)
> Museo de Historia de Valencia (p107)

TAPAS

Tradition tells that king Alfonso X, known as Il Sabio (The Wise), introduced this excellent custom back in the 13th century. Aware of the effect of alcohol upon an empty stomach, he decreed that no wine should be served without food. So tavern owners adopted the tradition of serving a modest portion of ham, chorizo or cheese. The small plate would be placed on top of the glass or carafe to 'tapar' (cover) it and keep out dust and flies. What's more probable if less romantic is that the practice originated in Andalucia's sherry-producing area in the 19th century and spread northwards.

Ir de tapeo or *tapear,* to go on a tapas crawl, isn't a particularly Valencian tradition. This said, almost every bar will have a selection of snacks to nibble and sample (but rare are the places where they come free, except, perhaps, for a saucer of olives or peanuts). Some places, whether traditional or ultracontemporary, specialise in tapas. For a larger portion, ask for a *ración;* for something in between, a *media ración.*

And take your tapas at the pace that suits your mood of the moment: an accompaniment to a glass of beer or wine; a snack before a main meal; or, as the plates stack up, a meal in itself. Be warned, though, that it's just as expensive – and indeed often more so – to dine on tapas as to eat à la carte. Well worth it, though, for the sheer variety of taste sensations, especially if you're sharing with friends.

BEST FOR TRADITIONAL TAPAS
> Bodega Casa Montaña (p92)
> Villaplana (p110)
> Ca'an Bermell (p40)
> Casa Guillermo (p92)
> Bodeguilla del Gato (p55)

BEST FOR MODERN TAPAS
> Sagardí (pictured above; p70)
> Tacita de Plata (p44)
> Pepita Pulgarcita (p43)
> La Drassana (p100)
> La Taberna de Marisa (p57)

GAY & LESBIAN VALENCIA

Compared with Madrid and Barcelona, Valencia's gay scene is a paler shade of pink. Even so, there's plenty of activity.

The Centro Histórico has two longstanding gay-friendly cafes. **Café de la Seu** (Map p47, D3; ☎ 96 391 57 15; C del Santo Cáliz 7; ⏱ 6pm-1.30 or 2am) is a relaxing place to enjoy a creative cocktail. **Café Sant Miquel** (Map p37, C3; ☎ 96 392 31 29; Plaza Sant Miguel 13; ⏱ noon-2am Oct-Jun, 9pm-midnight Jul-Sep) has a broad summertime terrace, does decent meals and, as night advances, morphs into a music bar.

Valencia's two main gay dance clubs are an easy walk from each other. **Deseo 54** (Map p97, A1; www.deseo54.com; C de Pepita 15; €10-12; ⏱ 1am-late Thu-Sun), just north of the river, normally plays a mix of electro and house. **Venial** (Map p37, C4; ☎ 96 391 73 56; www.venialvalencia.com; C Quart 26; ⏱ 1-7.30am Thu-Sun), particularly popular with the younger crowd, also has a chill-out zone and is big on cabarets.

Som Com Som (Map p83, D3; ☎ 96 332 66 48; C de Cádiz 75; ⏱ 8pm-2.30am) in Russafa is a friendly girls bar where you can throw darts, play billiards or just sip a coffee or copa.

Of Valencia's several gay saunas, **Sauna Magnus** (Map p97, C4; ☎ 96 337 48 92; Av del Puerto 27; €14; ⏱ 10am-midnight) is indeed on the grand scale with pool, hot tub, equally hot videos and private cabins.

Informative gay websites include www.gayvalencia.org (in Spanish), www.gayiberia.com/Valencia and http://guia.universogay.com/Valencia (in Spanish), with a useful click-on map.

MODERN VALENCIAN ARCHITECTURE

Architecturally, there's much more to Valencia than its historic heart. Although most construction sites are currently dormant because of the economic crisis, some stunning new buildings have been thrown up in the last two decades.

The Palau de la Música, completed in 1987, was the first of Valencia's monumental scale contemporary buildings. Mirrored in the artificial lake beneath, it looks for all the world like a giant greenhouse. Nicknamed the *microondas* (microwave), it can feel like one too in summer.

Most striking of all are the Santiago Calatrava creations for the City of Arts & Sciences (p10). From this space-age complex, two structures stand out: the sheer, imposing bulk of the Palau de les Arts and, soaring sky-wards, the Puente del Assut d'Or, Calatrava's latest contribution. The City has been a catalyst for massive new development all around as tall, truly creative apartment blocks mix it with more mundane structures.

Valencia's Palacio de Congresos (1999), like the City of Arts & Sciences, has been an impetus for exciting architectural developments in a previously dull suburb. Designed by British architect Sir Norman Foster, it has seeded a minor forest of tall office and residential structures and cutting-edge new hotels.

The city's investment in transport has been massive in recent years. Most evident are the new bridges flung across the riverbed. Look underground too, at the stations of the city's ever-expanding metro system. In particular, a visit to the cavernous Alameda stop beneath Puente de la Exposición (both Calatrava creations) is like descending into the skeleton of a whale.

BEST CONTEMPORARY ARCHITECTURE
> Palau de les Arts (p10)
> Hemisfèric (p10)
> Veles e Vents (p92)
> Palacio de Congresos (p108)
> Museo de las Ciencias Príncipe Felipe (p10)

NEWEST BRIDGES
> Puente de las Flores (Map p97, B3)
> Puente de la Exposición (Map p97, B3)
> Puente del Assut d'Or (Map p97, D5)
> Puente del Reino (Map p97, B4)
> Puente de Monteolivete (Map p97, C5)

Courtyard in the Palacio del Marqués de Dos Aguas (p62)

BACKGROUND

HISTORY

Valencia's first known permanent settlement was established in 138 BC, when Roman legionnaires were granted prime riverside land to build themselves a retirement community, which they named 'Valentia'. As Roman Imperial power waned, the town was scarcely touched by the Visigoth invasions from north of the Pyrenees, which had a major impact upon the rest of the Spanish peninsula.

The influence of the Muslims was much more fundamental and long-standing. Arabs established the still-extant ceramics industry of Manises and Paterna west of Valencia and improved irrigation techniques. They also introduced the water wheel, rice (still grown around the Albufera freshwater lagoon) and oranges, the region's most important contemporary cash crop.

The legendary Castilian knight El Cid briefly interrupted Muslim rule in 1094, but nearly a century and a half were to pass before the Christian king Jaime I and his troops from the north definitively retook the city in 1238. The

EL CID, SOLDIER OF FORTUNE

The romantic figure of El Cid shines through history as the brave Christian knight who, fighting for faith and king, threw back the Muslim invader. It's a stereotype reinforced by the 1961 Hollywood blockbuster with Charlton Heston as El Cid atop his trusty warhorse Babieca (among the film's picturesque, if apocryphal, episodes of derring-do: his catapulting food to the starving citizens of Valencia). The legend began soon after his death in 1099 and was further embellished and sanitised and reinforced in *El Cantar de Mio Cid* (The Song of the Cid), Spain's greatest epic poem, composed around a century later.

The reality's rather different. El Cid was born Rodrigo Díaz, son of a minor nobleman from Burgos in northern Spain. Operating along the moving, unstable frontier between Muslim-occupied Spain and lands reoccupied by the forces of the Reconquista, he shifted alliances and transferred his loyalties with political acumen worthy of any contemporary Afghan warlord. Appointed standard bearer by King Sancho II of Castile, he coolly switched his allegiance to Sancho's usurper Alfonso VI of Léon. Banished by his new patron for independently attacking the Muslim fiefdom of Toledo, at the time under Alfonso's protection, he sold his services to another Muslim, Yusuf al Mutamin, ruler of Zaragoza. Alfonso, recognising El Cid's military genius, recalled him from exile for the campaign against Muslim-held Valencia, which El Cid, as in all his battlefield initiatives, conducted as a personal campaign for personal gain. In this, he was no different from many of his contemporaries; just more successful.

ruler's most important legacy to Valencia was its Fueros charter guaranteeing the region considerable independence from the crown of Aragón.

GOLD TURNS TO DUST

Valencia enjoyed its *siglo de oro* (golden age) in the 15th century, 200 years before the rest of Spain. At this time, it was one of the Mediterranean's strongest trading centres. Commerce brought wealth and the magnificent La Lonja silk exchange, the Palau de la Generalitat, the cathedral's Miguelete bell tower and the protective Torres de Quart were constructed. However, in 1492, the very year in which the Moors lost Granada, their last foothold in Spain, all Jews were expelled from Spain, leaving Valencia bereft of many of its most important financiers and skilled artisans. The impact of this forced relocation, however, was nothing compared with the early-17th-century expulsion of the Moriscos, Muslims who had remained in the region after the Reconquista. In just five years an estimated 170,000 souls left by sea. Much of the interior was severely underpopulated and a whole social layer of craftspeople and water managers was skimmed off. The middle classes too were affected – to such an extent that in 1613 the Banco Municipal de Valencia went bankrupt. Reeling from such blows, the Valencia region, which for two centuries had outshone Catalonia, lost a superiority that it was never again to recover.

Like Catalonia, Valencia backed the wrong horse in the War of the Spanish Succession (1702–13) and in retribution Bourbon king Felipe V abolished Valencia's Fueros. A century later, in 1812, Valencia suffered again when French forces under Marshal Suchet besieged and occupied the city.

INDUSTRY & WARS

In the 19th century, Valencia's silk industry employed more than 25,000 workers, until it was decimated by a combination of disease and competition from Lyon in France. Wool from the interior was also exported through the city. Of even greater significance for the landscape today, citrus farming expanded and tonne upon tonne of oranges destined for France, the UK and Germany were exported through Valencia's port.

Although Spain did not participate in WWI, the Comunidad Valenciana was hit hard economically. When Germany began to blockade boats bearing oranges to enemy countries, whole orchards were ripped out. Sales of wine from the region slumped too. Only the trade in rice, imported by all sides as a food staple, remained buoyant.

BACKGROUND

When, on 17 July 1936, General Francisco Franco led the army in his Nationalist uprising that sparked the Spanish Civil War, Valencia unanimously opted for the Republican cause. In November, as the Nationalist noose around Madrid was tugged tighter, the Republican government – the legally elected government – moved to the city, decamping to Barcelona just under a year later. In 1939, Valencia and Alicante were the last loyal cities to be overcome by nationalist forces.

HARD TIMES

General Franco kept Spain out of WWII and the country subsequently suffered a UN-sponsored boycott. The years that followed are known as the *años de hambre* (years of hunger). Only in the late 1950s did Valencia return to pre–Civil War economic levels. From then on, progress was steady and swift. Even so, thousands of *valencianos* crossed the Pyrenees, seeking work in more prosperous countries such as France, Germany and Switzerland. Internally, a shorter migration route led from the region's interior to Valencia city and coastal resorts, leaving much of the interior underpopulated.

A REGION REBORN

With the death of Franco in 1975, regionalism once more became respectable and Valencia was formally declared an autonomous region in 1982. The Fueros may not have been restored but, benefiting from the decentralisation that followed Franco's death, Valencia and its region today enjoy a high degree of self-government. The Valencian language too, thanks to a regional TV station and compulsory courses at school level, has become for many a source of regional pride.

Regional self-confidence has generated a remarkable number of major urban projects such as the Metro network, the City of Arts & Sciences, the Palacio de Congresos, a major European conference venue, the clean-sweep revamping of the port area and, to the north of town, the Ricardo Tormo motor-racing circuit. Valencia has also reached out – some citizens would say overreached itself – to attract major international events such as the 2007 America's Cup yachting races and the European Grand Prix Formula One motor race that whines around the port each August. These days, the city, in common with the rest of Europe, is feeling the pinch, construction cranes stand idle, tourism revenues are down and the municipality is massively in debt. But the self-confidence is there, the willingness to think big, ready in waiting for when the economy picks up again.

NOISE

Spain, it's attested, is the world's noisiest country after Japan — and in Valencia the decibel counter runs at its highest. Much of it is traffic din on busy highways. But a great deal is human too, especially at bar throwing-out time. It's a divisive social issue. Bar owners say they do their best, keep their doors closed and display notices asking customers to respect their neighbours' right to sleep. Ravers out to enjoy their weekend resent recent legislation that requires music bars to close at 3.30am. And residents complain bitterly about the human racket. One drastic action has been to declare an area of bars and clubs a *zona acústica saturada*, embargoing any new bars and imposing severe restrictions on existing premises. But it's no solution; the partyers move on, the zone dies and everyone loses.

LIFE IN VALENCIA

The people of the Levante, as this stretch of Mediterranean coast is commonly called, have a reputation for being joyous, convivial and noisy, traits that find their expression in the Las Fallas festival (p130). They're great eaters out who like to stay out late. Like most Spaniards, they prefer their pleasures away from home, as you'll quickly discover if you're out and about any night between Wednesday and Saturday. The obverse of this is that you can know people very well yet never have entered their home. By contrast, for many *valencianos*, both young and old, the family is the pivot of their social life with meals, holidays and outings all taken together.

Many Valencians have a second home, either a villa or the traditional family house, within reasonable driving distance, to which they take off on summer weekends (some of the city's most spectacular traffic jams are of cars crawling back into town late on Sunday evenings) and during August.

ENVIRONMENT

Water, its present supply and future demands upon it, is an increasing preoccupation. And Valencia's wish to claim a share of diverted waters from the River Ebro, which runs through both Aragón and Catalonia, is a constant source of tension with its northern neighbours. Even so, the streets of the city are sluiced down nightly with thousands of litres of water, mostly recycled, that gurgles away down drains.

On the plus side, although *valencianos* grumble, their city has an excellent integrated public transport system. Most buses have disabled access and an increasing number run on natural gas or recycled cooking oil.

VALENCIA'S TWO LANGUAGES

Valencia and its region have two official languages: Spanish (often called *castellano*, a word derived from Castilia, Spain's heartland on the high central plain) and *valenciano*. Almost everyone is at ease speaking Spanish and increasing numbers of Valencians – particularly younger ones, who've studied it as a compulsory subject in school – handle the local language comfortably as well.

According to strict linguistic criteria, *valenciano* is a dialect of Catalan, a language shared with Catalonia and many in Andorra and the Balearic Islands. But the linguistic dimension is only one of many and language is always an emotive topic. For the right and folkloric end of the political spectrum, *valenciano* is a distinct language with its own norms, grammar and literature. By contrast, those on the left are content to consider it as a dialect of Catalan, on equal terms with it.

Quite a lot of *valencianos* hold firm opinions on the role of the Valencian language, and also the region's relations with Catalonia and the central government. Unless you know those you're talking with well, you're probably better off just nodding sympathetically.

Even so, it's difficult to prise car owners from their beloved vehicles, main arteries get clogged and parking can induce apoplexy.

GOVERNMENT & POLITICS

Confusing stuff but Valencia city is the principal town and capital of Valencia province, which in its turn fits within the Comunidad Valenciana (Valencia region) – of which Valencia city is also the capital. These days, the Comunidad Valenciana, one of 17 semiautonomous regions of Spain, enjoys a degree of control over its affairs that it hasn't had since 1707, when its Fueros, special privileges granted when the city was recovered from the Muslims, were abrogated. The Ayuntamiento (Town Hall, the organ of municipal government) has the greatest impact upon citizens' everyday lives. Both at present are in the hands of the right-wing Partido Popular, re-elected in 2008. Since the national government in Madrid is controlled by the PSOE (Partido Socialista Obrero Español), there's frequent bickering, accusation and counter-accusation between central and Valencian regional organs.

THE ARTS
PAINTING

Valencia's first painter of lasting renown was Juan de Juanes (c 1500–79), whose sensitive mannerist canvases with their bright patches of colour still decorate many a parish church around the region. From the 17th century, when artists such as Velázquez, Murillo and Zurbarán were active elsewhere in Spain, sprang two local artists who can hold their own with the greatest. Francisco Ribalta (1564–1628) influenced a whole generation of artists through his Valencia studio and school. Among his altarpieces with their strong interplay of light and shade is his *San Francisco abrazado al crucificado* (San Francisco embracing the crucified Jesus) in Valencia's Museo de Bellas Artes (p20). José de Ribera (1591–1652), renowned for his forceful realism, just manages to squeeze in as a scion of Valencia even though in his early twenties he moved to southern Italy, at the time ruled by Spain, where he was known as *il spagnoletto,* the little guy from Spain.

In the second half of the 19th century, artists of what is loosely called the Valencian Impressionist school worked largely to commission, turning out landscapes, portraits that flatter, peasants and fisherfolk, viewed with a somewhat romantic eye. Ignacio Pinazo (1849–1916; see p14) in his portraiture captured with broad brushstrokes the essence of a subject's character. José Benlliure (1855–1937) records popular traditions and half-recalled customs – a farm worker puffing at a pipe or a peasant with his flask of wine. You can visit his studio (p38).

Joaquín Sorolla (1863–1923), the most famous Valencian who subscribed to the Impressionist school, also dug deep into the daily life of everyday folk for much of his inspiration. Known as 'the painter of light', he portrays its transient flicker upon water. He too did his share of portraits for hard cash, fixing on canvas prominent personalities from Valencian society of the day.

MUSIC

Remember *Rodrigo's Guitar Concerto,* originally composed for guitar and orchestra and subsequently adapted in just about every musical mode? Known in Spanish as the *Concierto de Aranjuez* it, and many other compositions, are the creation of Joaquín Rodrigo (1901–99), born in Sagunto (p120) and Valencia's most famous musical son.

If you're around Valencia and its region in summer or during Fallas, you'll probably hear the sound of a *banda,* a good old-fashioned brass band, often supplemented with wind instruments such as flutes, clarinets and even saxophones. It's a tradition that began in the 18th century and almost every *barrio* (district) and village can boast one. Blowing at any street parade or fiesta, the quality varies from alarmingly wheezy to very professional indeed and competition is cutthroat at Valencia's annual *banda* championships, which coincide with its July summer festival.

DANCE

The city has a particularly active contemporary dance scene with visiting companies and its own permanent troupe, the Ballet de Teatres de la Generalitat, giving regular performances in the Teatro Principal and at the annual Sagunto festival. Valencia's most famous dancer and chore-ographer, Nacho Duarte, in his time principal dancer with the UK's Royal Ballet and Australian Ballet, nowadays directs Spain's Compañia Nacional de Danza (National Dance Company).

ARCHITECTURE

The three distinct portals of Valencia's cathedral (p12) give a rapid overview of how the Romanesque, Gothic and baroque each manifested itself in local ecclesiastical architecture. Mediterranean Gothic's most exuberant flourishing, by contrast, was in the temporal rather than spiritual domain. Coinciding with Valencia's 15th-century golden age, it informs monumental public buildings such as La Lonja (p18), the Palau de la Generalitat (p39) and the cathedral's emblematic Miguelete bell tower.

The Renaissance reached Valencia from Italy earlier than elsewhere in much of Spain (the infamous Borgia family, ensconced in Rome and the Vatican, came from Gandía, just down the coast) but it was of relatively minor architectural importance. The baroque had an altogether more profound impact. Few churches were constructed from scratch in ba-roque style. However, coinciding with another time of economic prosper-ity for the city, many were embellished with elaborate facades and ornate *retablos,* huge gilded, painted altarpieces that dwarf the altar itself. From this period too comes the magnificent octagonal tower of the church of Santa Catalina (p49), soaring skywards above the original Gothic place of worship, and also the extravagant rococo excess of the marble facade of the Palacio del Marqués de Dos Aguas (p62).

The restatement of classical architectural principles that informs much 19th-century Spanish architecture is evident in many of the bourgeois domestic buildings of L'Eixample. By far the most significant public build-ing from this time is the Plaza de Toros (Bullring), a vast, colonnaded, symmetrical and deeply pleasing structure. Neoclassical too in their con-

SANTIAGO CALATRAVA'S SINUOUS CONCRETE STRUCTURES

International architect Santiago Calatrava, born and educated in Valencia, designs mainly public projects such as bridges, stations, museums and stadiums — creations to be experienced by thousands of people every day. You'll recognise his grand-scale structures immediately, his signature as distinctive and easily recognised as the Coca-Cola logo. Technologically, he pushes to the limits what can balance, counter, take and impart stress in concrete, iron and steel. For Valencia, Calatrava is as significant as Gaudí remains for Barcelona. The Catalan's use of *trencadí* (slivers-of-broken-tile mosaic) and his fluid forms based upon nature have been a major influence upon his Valencian successor. Calatrava's soaring structures, all sinuous white curves with scarcely a right angle in sight, also relate to things organic: the vast blinking eye of the Hemisféric or the filigree struts, like veins on a leaf, of the Umbracle, a vast, shaded walkway in the Ciudad de las Artes y las Ciencias.

In Valencia, most of the City of Arts & Sciences is his design, including the very latest dramatic creation, the multifunctional space of the Agora. Drop beneath the Puente de la Exposición to the Alameda metro station with its soaring struts and bold curves. In the Basque country, his Volantín footbridge complements Bilbao's famous Guggenheim Museum nearby. In the US, he designed the Milwaukee Art Museum on the shores of Lake Michigan and is the architect of the transportation terminal for the new World Trade Center site in New York. And sports fan may recall his eyecatching steel and glass dome for the main stadium of the Athens Olympic games. More recent and more angular is his Turning Torso Tower in Malmö, Sweden, while two hugely ambitious projects in the US — 80 South St, a cuboid residential development in New York, and the 615m-high Chicago Spire, destined to be the tallest building in North America, are currently on hold, pending refinancing.

fidence and clean lines are Valencia's resplendent town hall and, facing it, the main post office (p62).

Altogether more original was Modernismo (a variant of art nouveau), an artistic movement that originated in Catalonia, to the north, and whose most famous proponent is Antoni Gaudí. See p115 for a one-hour walking tour that highlights Valencia's best, including the splendid Estación del Norte (p74), Mercado Central (p50) and Mercado de Colón (p74).

Contemporary architect, Valencia-born Santiago Calatrava (above), picks up the traditions of Modernismo with its favouring of *trencadí* (slivers-of-broken-tile mosaic) and shapes deriving from nature. Creating primarily in supple, malleable concrete, a material denied to those of an earlier era, his bridges and creations for the architecturally stunning City of Arts & Sciences (p10) have had a major impact upon the city in the last two decades.

DIRECTORY
TRANSPORT
ARRIVAL & DEPARTURE
AIR

At the time of writing, these operators flew to/from the UK and major European cities:

Air Europa Paris (Charles de Gaulle)
Clickair Milan (Malpensa), Paris (Orly), Rome
EasyJet London (Gatwick), Bristol
Flybaboo Geneva
Ryanair London (Stansted), Nottingham (East Midlands), Brussels (Charleroi)
Vueling Amsterdam, Brussels

In summer, Delta Airlines flies directly to/from New York (JF Kennedy).

Arriving in Valencia
Metro lines 3 and 5 (single/return ticket €1.90/3.30) connect the airport and city centre in less than 30 minutes.

AIR TRAVEL ALTERNATIVES
If time's not a factor, consider a more leisurely arrival by rail. Fast trains run between Valencia and both Madrid and Barcelona, from where there are connections to major European cities. From London, Eurostar (www.eurostar.com) whisks you to Paris, with connections to both cities.

A taxi into the centre costs around €17 (there's a supplement of €2.50 for journeys originating at the airport).

GETTING AROUND
The most active part of Valencia is delightfully compact and most places are within easy walking distance of each other.

TRAVEL PASSES
Valencia Tourist Card (☎ 900 70 18 18; per day/2 days/3 days €10/16/20) gives

---

CLIMATE CHANGE & TRAVEL
Travel – especially air travel – is a significant contributor to global climate change. At Lonely Planet, we believe that all who travel have a responsibility to limit their personal impact. As a result, we have teamed with Rough Guides and other concerned industry partners to support Climate Care, which allows people to offset the greenhouse gases they are responsible for with contributions to energy-saving projects and other climate-friendly initiatives in the developing world. Lonely Planet offsets all staff and author travel.

For more information, turn to the responsible travel pages on www.lonelyplanet.com. For details on offsetting your carbon emissions and a carbon calculator, go to www.climatecare.org.

unlimited travel by public transport and entitles you to discounts at lots of sights, restaurants and shops. Pick one up from participating hotels, some *estancos* (tobacconists) or offices of Turismo Valencia.

A 10-journey Bono Bus costs €6. Passes that are valid for one day (T1; €3.50), two days (T2; €6) or three days (T3; €8.60) allow you to have unlimited travel on bus, tram and metro. For each, you need to purchase a Móbilis, a touch-sensitive, rechargeable card (€2) sold at major metro stations, most *estancos* as well as some newspaper kiosks.

BICYCLE HIRE
Do You Bike (Map p47, B3; ☎ 96 315 55 51; www.doyoubike.com; Plaza del Horno de San Nicolás) Has a couple more outlets around town.

Orange Bikes (Map p61, B2; ☎ 96 391 75 51; www.orangebikes.net; C del Editor Manuel Aguilar 1)

Valencia Guías (Map p105, B3; ☎ 96 385 17 40; www.valenciaguias.com; Paseo de la Pechina 32)

BUS
EMT (☎ 96 352 83 99; www.emtvalencia.es) buses run until about 10pm. Night services continue on nine routes until around 3am. A single journey costs €1.25.

CAR HIRE
In Valencia city, a car is an encumbrance. For exploring beyond, inexpensive local companies renting at Valencia airport include:
Javea Cars (☎ 96 579 33 12; www.javea cars.com)
Solmar (☎ 96 153 90 42; www.solmar.es)
Victoria Cars (☎ 96 583 02 54; www .victoriacars.com)

GETTING AROUND TOWN

	Plaza de la Virgen	Port & Beach	City of Arts & Sciences	Bioparc	IVAM
Plaza de la Virgen	n/a	bus 25min	bus 15min	bus 20min	walk 15min
Port & Beach	bus 25min	n/a	walk 20min	tram & metro 40min	tram 30min
City of Arts & Sciences	bus 15min	walk 20min	n/a	bus 25min	bus 15min
Bioparc	bus 20min	tram & metro 40min	bus 25min	n/a	walk 20min, bus 10min
IVAM	walk 15min, bus 10min	tram 30min	bus 15min	walk 20min, bus 10min	n/a

STREET SIGNS

Street signs are, increasingly, only in *valenciano*. However, Spanish is the language that every local understands and most use. So we do too – for addresses and also on maps, where we occasionally cite the *valenciano* alternative as well, when it's markedly different from the Spanish.

METRO & TRAM

Metrovalencia (☎ 900 46 10 46; www .metrovalencia.com) runs the combined metro and high-speed tram network. A one/two/ three/four-zone journey costs €1.40/1.90/2.60/3.60. Buy from machines at any station. Services run between about 6am and 11pm.

TAXI

Call **Radio-Taxi** (☎ 96 370 33 33) or **Valencia Taxi** (☎ 96 357 13 13). A green light on the roof or a *libre* sign indicate that a taxi's available. The minimum fare is €3.80 (€6 between 10pm and 6am).

PRACTICALITIES
BUSINESS HOURS

Banks (8.30am-2pm Mon-Fri; some also open 4-7pm Thu & 9am-1pm Sat)
Main Post Office (8.30am-8.30pm Mon-Fri, 9.30am-2pm Sat)
Offices (8am or 9am-2pm & 4-7pm or 5-8pm Mon-Fri)

Restaurants (2-4pm & 9pm-midnight; most close one day per week)
Shops (10am-2pm & 5-8pm Mon-Sat; many big stores & supermarkets don't close at lunchtime)

INTERNET

Extra Valencia (http://extravalencia.com) A little bland but good for what's on and extensive general information.
Hola Valencia (www.holavalencia.net) Engagingly written, finger on the city's pulse. Has great photos.
This is Valencia (www.thisisvalencia.com) Reliable and longest running of the privately maintained local websites.
Visual Valencia (www.visualvalencia.com) Virtual tours of major city sites and more.

For tourist office websites, see p152.

Conveniently central, **Work Center** (Map p61, D4; Calle Xàtiva 19; per hr €3; ⏰ 24hr Mon-Thu, 7am-11pm Fri, noon-2pm & 5-9pm Sat & Sun) has internet access.

MONEY

Spain's currency is the euro (€). For credit card payments, some shops ask for photo ID. At modest hotels and restaurants, check in advance whether plastic's accepted.

COSTS

Spain's cost of living is generally less than elsewhere in western Europe, though the difference is ever less marked. Public transport is cheap and taxi rates, though climbing upwards, remain reasonable. You can still get a simple *menú del día* (midday special) for €12 as well as an excellent lunch for €20.

NEWSPAPERS & MAGAZINES

Turia is a comprehensive weekly what's on guide in Spanish. Long-established monthlies *24/7* and **Valencia Connect** (www.valenciaconnect .com), available in tourist offices and major tourist outlets, are the best of the freebie guides in English.

ORGANISED TOURS

Art Valencia (☎ 96 310 61 93; www.art valencia.com) Two-hour walking tours (€7.50) departing 11am Friday from the Plaza de la Reina tourist office.

Orange Bikes (Map p61, B2; ☎ 96 391 75 51; www.orangebikes.net; C del Editor Manuel Aguilar 1) Bespoke guided cycle tours, minimum two people.

Paseando Valencia (☎ 656 359504; www .paseandovalencia.es) Two-hour dramatised tours of the Centro Histórico in Spanish (€14; 10pm Saturday, March to October).

Turiart (☎ 96 352 07 72; www.turiart.com) Two-hour walking tours (€12) departing 11am Sunday from C de Caballeros 7.

Valencia Guías (Map p105, B3; ☎ 96 385 17 40; www.valenciaguias.com; Paseo de la Pechina 32) Daily 3½-hour guided bicycle tours in English (€25 including rental; minimum two people), leaving from its premises at 10am. Also two-hour walking tours in Spanish and English (adult/child €15/7.50), leaving the

Plaza de la Reina tourist office at 10am each Saturday.

TELEPHONE

For international calls you'll get lots more chat from a cut-rate scratch card, sold by *locutorios* (call centres), plus many *estancos* and newsstands. Most *locutorios* also offer cut-rate overseas calls.

MOBILE PHONES

Spain uses the GSM mobile (cellular) phone system, compatible with most phones, except those sold in Japan and the US. Using your home mobile phone is expensive; if your phone's unblocked, consider slipping in a Spanish SIM card (from around €10).

USEFUL PHONE NUMBERS

International directory enquiries
☎ 11825
International operator – Europe & Morocco ☎ 1008
International operator – rest of the world ☎ 1005
Local directory inquiries ☎ 11818

AUDIOGUIDE

Turismo Valencia rents out multilingual MP3 audioguides (per half-day/day €5/7.50) from its Plaza de la Reina and Estación del Norte branches. Be sure to return yours on time; late returns rack up a surcharge of €5 per hour.

TIPPING

In restaurants, most *valencianos* leave small change or around €1 per person. Taxi drivers don't expect a tip but rounding up gets a smile. At top-end hotels, tip the porter €2 to €5.

TOURIST INFORMATION

Regional tourist office (Map p61, F2; ☎ 96 398 64 22; www.comunitatvalenciana .com; C de la Paz 48; ⏰ 9am-8pm Mon-Fri, 10am-8pm Sat, 10am-2pm Sun) Its excellent website covers the city and region.

Turismo Valencia (VLC) tourist office (www.turisvalencia.es) Plaza de la Reina (Map p47, D3; ☎ 96 315 39 31; Plaza de la Reina 19; ⏰ 9am-7pm Mon-Sat, 10am-2pm Sun); Airport (☎ 8.30am-8.30pm Mon-Fri, 9.30am-5.30pm Sat & Sun); Estación del Norte (main station, C Xàtiva; ⏰ 9am-7pm Mon-Sat, 10am-2pm Sun); Las Arenas (Paseo de Neptuno 2; ⏰ 10am-7pm Mon-Fri, 10am-6pm Sat & Sun); Town Hall (Plaza del Ayuntamiento; ⏰ 9am-7pm Mon-Sat, 10am-2pm Sun) Also at the ferry terminal when cruise ships are in harbour.

TRAVELLERS WITH DISABILITIES

Some hotels and public institutions have wheelchair access. Most buses have descending ramps and most metro stations have escalators.

>INDEX

See also separate subindexes for Do (p156), Drink (p156), Eat (p157), Play (p158), See (p158) and Shop (p159).

🏃 **DO**

🍸 **DRINK**

000 map pages

000 map pages